The Global Nomad

ISBN: 9798986528076 Softcover
Printed in the United States of America

Published: January 2024

For information about this title or to order books and/or electronic media, contact the publisher:
Sula Too Publishing
www.sulatoo.com/publishing
813-200-8878

Calvin Campbell

The Global Nomad

Footprints Across Continents

Calvin Campbell

Sula Too
Publishing

The Global Nomad

Calvin Campbell

Table of Contents

Calvin Campbell

I've Been Many Places And Seen Many Things

My desire to travel was pushed into reality by my wish to leave home and the Bronx. I had lived there all my life and had never felt as if I belonged. I was an outsider in my neighborhood. I was tall, lanky with no swag, no dress style or flavor. I spoke with a stutter and had worn glasses since a little kid. I definitely wasn't the most popular teenager, simply tolerated as I tried hard to blend in and not make waves. Looking back these two traits opened amazing

Figure 1 Freelance work in Tampa International Plaza

7

opportunities for me and gave me an interesting life.

At age 18, my first tiny steps were moving myself to Manhattan. I had taken the train into the city a few times, and knew I liked Greenwich Village. So, I got a job and saved enough money to afford a room share, and then gave myself a couple of weeks to find work in that neighborhood.

It went well for me. I met an older man and his partner who became my friends and mentors. I really needed to be shown the ropes as life in Greenwich Village was so different and very liberating. People were from all walks of life and from all over the world, it became more of an eye opener than I realized and with the help of my mentors I came to terms with myself.

As I became more confident, I started to think about California. The Freedom Movement was tugging at me, I wanted to be part of it. I was encouraged by my friends to experience the big world out there. So, I said goodbye to them and my family, bought a one-way ticket, rode the Greyhound bus, and finally arrived in San Francisco, California four days later.

Why Write A Book?

As a guy born in Harlem, who grew up in the South Bronx, and because of being frequently asked about my motivation for writing a book, I took the time to reflect on it. I came to the realization that travel and adventure are integral parts of my life journey, and my passion for them is what fuels my writing. My desire to leave a legacy for the next generation drives me to share my story, which is  not intended to boost my ego or bring me fame and glory. I am not attempting to be clever with this book venture; rather, it is simply the most effective way for me to communicate my experiences.

Throughout my travels, I have encountered numerous individuals who professed their care for me, only to disappear from my life. Though this has been a challenging experience, I have managed to maintain my hope, joy, and faith. Above all, the journey has been incredibly surreal and exciting, and as a result, I have not lost my trust in others or my immense gratitude.

As I traveled to foreign countries, I couldn't help but be grateful. As a guy from the Bronx, I often wondered how I ended up in such incredible places. Whenever this thought crossed my mind, I would simply smile and say a prayer of thanks.

One such moment occurred in the Egyptian desert as I looked up at the stars and the full moon. In that moment, I felt overwhelming gratitude for the grace of God and the universe. They had helped me through countless magical situations that were so surreal, I had to pinch myself to make sure I was aware.

I've been to so many countries, that I really had to stop and say, "How did I get here?" Because I always think I'm from New York. I'm from the Bronx, born in Harlem. Here I am, in Romania, or in Saint Petersburg, Russia. How did I get here? But it's only by God and the universe that allowed me to have this journey and protection to do these things and I am grateful.

One of the reasons for writing this book is because I've been so blessed and highly favored, that being an outsider allowed me to follow my dreams, passions, and imagination. The universe did the rest. God and the universe really held my hand and navigated me through life.

When I was very young, I didn't fit into the group in my neighborhood. I was a loner. Throughout my life, being a loner has been a significant aspect of my identity. Fortunately, through my travels, I have been able to make good friends all over the world. These individuals care about me for who I am and support my passions and interests. However, it can be challenging to share my experiences with people who do not share my interests. I have encountered many lovely and attractive individuals, but without shared interests, a deep connection is difficult to develop. This has been a recurring theme in my life.

Another essential aspect of my story is my passion for travel itself. While many people may express a desire to travel with me, they often lack the same level of passion that I have. Some individuals have even expressed negative attitudes toward my love of travel, but I have refused to let that stop me. To embark on a journey like mine, you must be adventurous, cutting-edge, and your own person. Nobody will feel the same passion for what you are doing as you do. As an outsider, I have come to realize that this is simply part of who I am.

I express gratitude towards God for the support I received from New York. My trips to Manhattan, where I explored the shops, visited Central Park and Greenwich Village, and interacted with people along the way, were delightful experiences. It helped me overcome the loneliness that comes with being a loner. One of the inspiring aspects of New York is the opportunity to meet people who have done things that you haven't done. Conversations with such people can inspire you to pursue your dreams.

As I met people from Los Angeles, San Francisco, Santa Barbara, and heard about places like Big Sur, Lake Carmel, and San Diego, I developed a strong desire to experience these places. However, I couldn't find anyone who shared my interest. I realized that my life was getting monotonous and boring with just a job to pay rent. So, I always asked God for protection and grabbed every opportunity that came my way, taking calculated risks.

As a risk-taker, I knew that even if the worst-case scenario happened, I would survive. When you are young, it is important to have this attitude because it opens many beautiful and magical experiences that you never thought could happen to you.

On some occasions, you might be invited to an amazing party where you have a blast. However, the following week, you may struggle to make ends meet and must settle for coffee and toast instead of indulging in fancy breakfast items. Being a risktaker comes with its challenges, but you must put your ego aside, refrain from being judgmental, and cherish the experience. When you reflect on life, all you have are memories of the fun times, the nerve-racking moments, and the times you had to make do. Loving yourself and having faith in God and the universe enables you to pursue your dreams and accomplish the seemingly impossible.

I believe that anyone can achieve their dreams, regardless of their background. Growing up in Harlem, living with my grandparents in Roanoke, Virginia, and attending Hunter College while working a job during the day at 42nd Street Library in Manhattan to pay the bills, I was just an ordinary person with a passion for social studies and world events.

I've been fortunate enough to travel to over 60 countries, staying in each for at least a month if it was worth it, or 14 days if it wasn't. I've even lived in 10 countries, in addition to the United States, where I've visited 13 of the most prominent and fascinating cities, from Las Vegas to San Francisco, from Detroit to Manhattan.

I come from a large supportive family in Roanoke Virginia, Spartanburg, South Carolina, and Savannah Georgia where my family holds our Family reunions and visits the cemetery where our ancestors dating back to the 1800s are buried. Still, I wanted to explore further. That's why I traveled to Africa, where I discovered that my ancestry can be traced back to West Africa, with some Scottish and Indian heritage in my family as well.

Despite not being the most studious or intellectual person, I followed my passions and took risks to achieve my dreams. And

I believe anyone else can do the same if they love themselves and have faith in God and the universe.

First Foreign Trip

I often get asked about my initial motivation for traveling and how I arranged my first trip, especially what inspired me to explore outside of the United States. When I reflect on this, I realize that growing up in New York, being a loner can be tough. The city provides company, but if you don't belong to the right crowd, you might feel uncomfortable even when hanging out with them. You crave a sense of belonging, but finding true companionship can be challenging. Being alone gives you time to contemplate what you want and where you fit in. I was always fond of traveling, but I didn't have any close friends who shared that interest. So, when things weren't working out for me in New York, I began to wonder where I would like to go if I were not in the United States. I considered the costs, logistics, and reception of different cultures.

Fortunately, my first trip abroad was a package deal to Nassau, which I was blessed to receive. I stayed at the Nassau Beach Hotel, where I enjoyed the beach, pool, and restaurant. I didn't venture far out of the resort since I was there for only seven days and six nights. However, I made friends with other hotel guests and attended various airline conventions and parties hosted on the hotel balconies. The trip was fun and exciting, and being able to plan and save for it successfully was a big achievement. Getting my passport and leaving the country for the first time felt adventurous and exhilarating. I didn't feel the need to explain or inform anyone; I just followed my free spirit and took advantage of the best deal I could find. Overall, my first trip was a great experience that sparked my love for travel and exploration.

After my first trip, I became addicted to travel and started searching high and low for similar experiences. The planning process itself was exhilarating and consumed my thoughts. The destination didn't matter as long as it was thrilling, whether it was England, Sweden, Russia, Spain, or Greece. The excitement of discovery and exploration coursed through me, and it was a love that replaced the one I never found.

Through travel, I learned to love and appreciate myself. I felt things and saw beauty that I didn't share with anyone else. Each journey helped me understand myself and the world around me better. I cherished the good times, which outnumbered the bad because of my outgoing nature. I would party with friends one day and then spend the next day with locals before mingling with upscale tourists at night.

As a bargain hunter, I always looked for the best deals in safe places, even if the country had problems. My curiosity about the Caribbean, Africa, and Europe's black communities made me want to be a citizen of the world and not stay in one place. I desired to be a visionary and spiritual person who could share and exchange ideas with people from all walks of life.

My spirituality is centered around giving, sharing, and receiving love, which allows me to interact with people, whether they look like me or not, share my culture or not. I'm interested in learning about their language, culture, and daily life. In tourist areas, there's often more English spoken, making communication easier.

For example, in Colombia where I stayed in Airbnb accommodations, where I would meet Germans, Americans, and Europeans. I explore the area during the day with locals, who give me a different perspective on life and make me appreciative of what I have. At night, I visit quaint architectural-style buildings and fusion restaurants, which add to the exotic atmosphere.

When I hook up with locals, it is understood that I must come out of pocket for food, transportation, and incidentals. I also plan tips, that may equate to a day's salary, for my local new friend and running buddy. Doing so means I get to experience places I wouldn't have found on my own. I love spending time with locals because they're authentic and give me a glimpse of their lives. A local's knowledge of the area allows us to go off the beaten track to adventurous hideaways. I don't judge them; instead, I appreciate them for who they are. It's a win/win situation.

Why I Travel Alone

As I continue to explore the world to see what it has to offer, my curiosity as a nomadic traveler has never stopped. With around 60 countries under my belt, with many of them repeat destinations. As of 2023, I have a 48-year friendship with someone who lives in Israel. If I count each time I visited him, my trips to Israel would account for 13 trips at one to three months on a tourist visa. Three months is the maximum time a tourist can stay, and I made good use of that time. I have lived in 10 countries outside the US, and 5 years in Hawaii. I have seen plenty. What follows is a partial list of some additional extraordinary places I have been:

*Germany found me working in a private Nightclub call "WHY NOT" who had world renowned musicians as customers, Mick Jagger, Billy Preston, etc. I spent two years having the time of my life and met a nomadic traveler hangout buddy who is still a good friend to this day.

*I have spent a lot of time in Brazil, from Rio de Janeiro (Brasília, Recife up to Salvador) all the way to Fortaleza. I also attended Ciranda, a spiritual music event held in the jungle about a two-hour ride outside of Rio. It is still one of my spiritual homes in the world where I first tried Ayahuasca with indigenous locals.

*Panama held my interest, so on the Island of Bastimentos I opened a guesthouse (Free Spirit Inn) that was in walking distance through Wizard the jungle to Wizard Beach and Red Frog Beach.

I loved it, but after six years I sold the property and moved on.

*Thailand was a favorite place for me, lots of nightlife, beautiful beaches and very easy going good-spirited people.

*Ghana clutched my heart, the center of the west coast African slave trade. Just being there seeing the inside of the original Cape Coast Castle and Elmina Castle filled me with emotion. I was devastated with the written history of The Door of No Return.

*Russia was diverse and interesting; I was two months immersed in the old imperial city of St. Petersburg. Four days checking out the Hermitage Museum, one of the largest in the world.

*Romania was like a fairy tale, the landscape, the university city of Cluj and country towns. I have gone back there many times. Great skiing, and the castle in Transylvania where Count Dracula lived is worth seeing.

*Egypt and Turkey were filled with history. I spent two years having adventures and exploring The Valley of the Kings in Egypt and learning the fabric and clothing manufacturing business in Turkey.

*Spain and Ibiza were definitely party places back in the day. Spending all summer with young mostly Europeans partying around the Mediterranean was always fun. The sea was warm, the food good the people from everywhere.

*I lived in North Cyprus in. Kyrenia, I had an apartment on the beach and stayed far too long. I decided to return to the States via Turkey, as it was the most direct shipping to Florida. Turkey was so great I stayed there for a year. Studying fabric and manufacturing unique men's formal wear fashion

*Colombia, I cannot keep myself away from Medellin the exotic city that truly never sleeps. I had to be careful, the fun part of the city for me was getting me in trouble, in a good way. I have been to Colombia six times visiting Cartagena, Medellin, and Bogota. Like me and ice cream I always want more!

I always wanted to see life's similarities and the differences to that of the USA, with all its complexities as a world power with a globally diverse population.

With changes over recent years, I'm finding out I'm not the only one with a nomadic spirit. I'm also starting to see more single women traveling mainly in Europe, Central and South America (which is great). I have seen them from all parts of the world moving around on their own, or in tourist groups. Mostly on group tours but also alone like me. They are a big part of the global community.

They are now looking to live outside their comfort zone, even if it means they must do it alone. Let me be clear, traveling alone can be an opportunity for them to be on their own without having to check with their partner about the type of adventures they want to have. Without negotiating the itinerary, on where, when, how, of known and unknown fears, which can be difficult to say the least. To agree on everything from where to go, first, places to stay, even where and what foods to eat can be a headache. Sometimes traveling alone or in tour groups offers the freedom to make spontaneous decisions without external input and gain confidence from making personal choices.

For me, when I travel, it helps me gain confidence by doing things my way, on my own terms, with my decisions based on letting my Spirit, God and my Energy play a part with my journey.

In hindsight, we sometimes regret the things we did not do, instead of what we did. Being a nomadic traveler with an adventurous spirit has created so many memories that put a smile on my face. Made me and others feel strong and happy. Made us have a full sense of accomplishment, for we did it our way. We did things that we wanted to experience outside of staying home and buying things we really didn't need.

I have found traveling alone helps make me become more sociable, to go outside of my comfort zone to make new connections. Traveling alone gives me more incentive to connect with people to foster a new relationship which sometimes become new friends. I'm blessed to have many friendships that were developed with people I met all around the world: Ghana, Ethiopia, Ivory Coast, Germany, Israel, Egypt, Brazil, Panamá, Colombia, Pakistan, France, Italy, Romania, Poland, Kenya, Turkey, Northern Cypress, as examples. Now, you are sharing stories with other locals who are interested in your culture and lifestyle or travelers along the way with their stories and experiences.

Some of them I most likely will never meet again. However, my time and spirit benefited from meeting so many people of different cultures, lifestyles, with such unique beauty. It has been fun, adventurous and with lots of memories.

Being a nomadic traveler most of my life, I developed a passion for adventurous and healthy curiosity. I now realize that life is too short not to allow my dreams to surface. A black global nomadic traveler on my own terms, learning and being my true self. There are those life changing experiences when I connect with my hopes and dreams to realize I'm a citizen of the world. That's not easy! I have had to deal with my fears, have difficult conversations with myself, push back on those fears and repressed desires, and stop complaining when things don't go my way.

As I realize that my experiences, good or bad, made me feel alive, strong in being my own individual person, and understanding that being alone and loving self can be fun. I know it is hard for some to understand how by traveling alone I fine is a confidence booster. I did it! Connecting with new people and places and their impact is what I share with people. The experiences I have had will stay with me for a lifetime because they helped me learn about the world around me. I would have never met my friends, contacts and having short intimate sweet relationships if I had stayed at home.

My insatiable curiosity as a nomadic traveler has never waned, even as I continue to explore the world and check off over 60 countries from my list. With decades of living in 10 countries outside the US and 5 years in Hawaii, I have observed the similarities and differences of cultures around the globe, especially as a citizen of a world power with a diverse population.

During my explorations over many years, I learned a great deal about myself. I have gained confidence and an appreciation of patience. Being from New York City, I needed to develop patience, which has not been easy for me. The friendships you make are unlike anything else, the feeling you get out of knowing you have connected with an individual who shares values and life views is amazing. It became one of the easiest ways to fully feel that you are no longer a tourist, you are neighbors looking out for each other.

I often say:
"You are a citizen of the world."

Travel Mentor

"Anyone who may wish to profit himself alone from the knowledge given him, rather than serve others through the knowledge he gained from learning, is betraying knowledge and rendering it worthless."

Emperor Haile Selassie

How Did I Get Here?

I am Calvin Campbell, and I was born in Harlem, New York to Calvin Sr. and Gladys Campbell. We moved to South Bronx when I was around nine years old, and it became my entire world until it was time to attend junior high school. Despite the school up the street, my parents opted to send me to a junior high school across town, where I had my first experience encountering people who looked different from me and were from other areas.

Later, my parents sent me to an all-boys sports high school, believing that it would be best for me. However, I faced a challenge from the beginning since I was not skilled in sports, had a speech impediment, and wore glasses. Even though I was tall and thin, I wasn't a basketball player. Despite being in a sports high school, I couldn't participate in track and field, even though I was relatively good at it. There seemed to be no suitable sport for me to engage in.

The topics that sparked my interest, such as world exploration and social studies, didn't attract most people. Additionally, I hung around with people who didn't look like me, mostly Jewish, Italian, or Irish. With them, I didn't feel the pressure to excel in sports or wear fashionable clothes as my parents provided me with clothes that lasted rather than being stylish. In our neighborhood, conformity was expected, especially among teenagers, and there were certain styles that we had to adopt unless we wanted to be outcasts. However, my parents didn't approve of this.

I started my new school at the age of 13 since my birthday was in the summer. One of my Jewish friends lived in Riverdale, New York, a predominantly white, Jewish area I had visited before, but I had some unpleasant experiences there. On one occasion, when I went to visit my friend, the doorman at his building refused to let me enter through the main door and instead directed me to the side entrance for deliveries. I shared this incident with my friends, and their parents were outraged, as they believed that such discrimination was unjustified.

One Sunday, my friends planned to go swimming at a nearby pool. When I arrived with my swimming trunks, there were about six of us ready to enjoy the pool. After my friends found us a spot to sit and relax, they jumped into the water. I was about to join them when I noticed parents telling their kids to leave the pool. I wasn't sure if it was because there were six of us or because of me specifically. The pool was quite large, so I thought it might be me. I had been having a great time until that moment, and suddenly the atmosphere changed. It puzzled and bothered me, but my friends were supportive and ignored it, as young kids often do.

I shared the incident at the pool with my parents. My stepmother, who was usually strict and believed in good manners, was upset, and said something that stuck with me, "I told you to be careful going around white people, because some of them will not treat you with respect." Her words stayed with me.

However, there was another occasion that had a different outcome. I had a good friend in Riverdale whose father was a dentist, and we used to go to his house to play music. We would listen to Chubby Checker and The Beatles. I was amazed at the freedom my friend had in his house. He could play loud music, go into the refrigerator, and get whatever he wanted, and had freedoms that I did not have. He helped me appreciate the type of freedom that was different from what most black kids experienced. My family was very strict, and I had to follow certain rules, such as saying "Yes, ma'am" and "No, ma'am", until I was 18 years old. Even after that, I was expected to be polite and respectful. This was the type of environment I grew up in.

At home, punctuality was highly valued. If dinner was scheduled for six o'clock, everyone was expected to be there at six. Father worked hard and we had to be home on time. Similarly, chores like cleaning your room were mandatory because your room was part of the house, and "You don't pay rent." as I was often told. I grew up with a lot of rules and regulations that my Jewish friends didn't have to worry about because they often had housekeepers who took care of such tasks. They had a more relaxed lifestyle where they could eat whenever they wanted, and Chinese food or pizza was often on the menu.

Initially, I felt envious of my Jewish friends' freedom, but I also recognized that my upbringing taught me the values of politeness and respect, which their parents appreciated. I understood that their different lifestyle was shaped by their unique environment.

What I cherished most about my upbringing was my belief in the saying, "I'm blessed, black, and highly favored," which always gave me hope. Even in the most stressful situations, God and the universe would eventually turn things around for me. Looking back, I found it special that even though my path was not always straight, I always ended up where I needed to be.

When my friend invited me to a Jewish synagogue in Riverdale, it was a magical experience. I went with him and his family to see Dr. Martin Luther King, who was visiting for a fundraiser for the Southern Christian Leadership Association. While my parents were happy for me, they were somewhat hesitant because there was considerable apprehension about what Dr. Martin Luther King was trying to do when he first gained popularity in the black community. With my parents' encouragement, I went to the synagogue dressed in my Sunday suit and made sure to mind my manners and not embarrass myself. Despite my apprehensions, I was thrilled to visit the synagogue and hear Dr. Martin Luther King speak, as I had never been to one before.

The synagogue was packed with only white people, and I was the only black person there. I wore my own yarmulke and sat in the middle with my friend's family. Dr. Martin Luther King was speaking, and I was impressed that so many white people had come to see and support a black man. It was a powerful moment that made me feel proud and special. When the assembly line started, I wanted to shake Dr. King's hand, but I was unsure of what to say. I greeted him and he greeted me back, and I left feeling elated.

Back in my neighborhood, I couldn't stop talking about the experience. While some people cared, it didn't seem to affect them as deeply as it did me. However, I remained engrossed in the world of Dr. Martin Luther King. I followed news coverage of the Freedom Riders and became aware of the violence and injustices faced by black people and their allies, from assassinations to imprisonments in the south. My parents cared, but they got over it quick. I was aware of when the two Jewish guys and a black guy were assassinated. I was aware of it all, the mishaps, evil, deaths, and imprisonment, from Selma to everywhere in the south.

At the time of the March on Washington, there was a concern that it could turn into a riot. Initially, both my stepmother and father said no when I asked for permission to attend. However, I persisted, and my father eventually agreed, given that I had relatives in Washington DC who I could stay with. I purchased a ticket and boarded a Greyhound bus filled with mostly black passengers. To my surprise, there was also a white kid on the bus who I ended up hanging out with. We navigated through the crowded event together, joining some 200,000 marchers in on the singing of songs like "We shall not, we shall not be moved." We tried our best to learn the lyrics and move from one area to the other where the singing was taking place.

The event drew people from all over the country, not just from the south as I had expected. It was a remarkable sight to witness so many black people gathered for this type of event. I made a conscious effort to listen to the various speakers and Dr. Martin Luther King's "I Have A Dream" speech. I was fascinated with Ralph Abernathy's civil rights organization story and with Andrew Young who spoke about Montgomery and Selma. The park between Lincoln Memorial and the Washington Monument for Civil Rights and Voter Rights was completely packed with people. We heard from many others whom I had read about or seen on TV.

I had a great passion for social studies, and many of my role models were present at the event. Even though I was only 14 years old at the time, it left a lasting impression on me that influenced my life forever. I became very aware of what was happening in my city, particularly in Manhattan where we attended church. On our way to church, we would see the black speakers on the corner of 125th Street and Lenox Avenue, including the Black Panthers. Parades for Daddy Grace, Father Devine, and Marcus Garvey, I even attended Abyssinia Baptist Church, the largest black church in New York City and one of the largest in the USA. Adam Clayton Powell Jr. was the pastor/politician who represented Harlem and other New York City neighborhoods in the House of Representatives.

Being a single guy without any siblings, I was quite nomadic. I developed a love for adventure and travel and would often take advantage of any free time I had to explore new places. Leaving the Bronx behind, I would venture into Manhattan to visit my cousin on 136th Street. However, my true purpose was to simply window shop and wander around with no specific agenda in mind. I was drawn to neighborhoods like Morningside Heights where there was a strong black community. Though I enjoyed my adventures, I had to be back home by a certain time, as my parents were strict about curfew.

There were also specific events and places that piqued my interest. I would visit my Jewish friends in Riverdale, but I wasn't always included in their larger events, especially if they involved girls. I was content hanging out with the guys over pizza and milkshakes or participating in after-school activities. However, when I sensed their energy shift, I knew it was time to head downtown to the village, where I felt welcomed and accepted for who I was.

My white schoolmates valued me as a person because I did not exhibit any signs of racism. However, I still felt excluded from certain events and activities because I wasn't Jewish. Sometimes, I would tag along with them to a friend's house after school, but there were moments of discomfort. For example, one time, my friend's mother asked me to look through the items they were throwing away, but I declined. They often made jokes about Sammy Davis Jr. because he was black and Jewish, but I wasn't a fan. I saw him and I knew that he had a white wife, Bridget from Scandinavia, or something like that. I was too young to really be involved in whatever he was doing.

It was hard to visit someone when you weren't invited or to hear people talking about events you weren't included in. I believe some of it had to do with their families or the people who would be at the events. It was hurtful, and it brought back my stepmother's warnings about dealing with "those white folks." I had to navigate my feelings.

I needed to have choices because staying in my neighborhood was not an option. Firstly, I didn't feel accepted there, and secondly, my parents were very controlling. They always wanted to know where I was going, where I had been, and where I was. Sometimes

I said I was going to the movies or some other place. But instead, I would go to places where I wanted to be.

One of my favorite places was Washington Square in Greenwich Village. People were gathered there, playing music loudly from speakers, juggling, rollerblading, and dancing. I loved the positive atmosphere and felt accepted. I spent a lot of my free time and Saturdays in that area.

When I started going out on weekends, I encountered difficulties with my parents because I often returned home after my curfew. This was since I had to take the slow Third Avenue L train in the Bronx, which would often cause me to be late. My stepmother would lock the door and chain it shut, forcing me to ring the bell and wake my father to let me in. My stepmother, who was the one responsible for locking the door, would purposely wait until my father had to get up then letting him know I was outside. She claimed to love me, but her actions made it clear that she cared more about my father, and I was simply a part of the package deal.

At times, being a part of the arrangement was simply unavoidable, and that was the case for me. My mother passed away when I was just six years old, and my grandparents came to New York to take me to Roanoke, Virginia, my father's hometown, which turned out to be a positive change. As a single man, my father couldn't juggle working and taking care of me. He worked as a longshoreman, unloading trucks at the waterfront, and we always had an abundance of fruits and vegetables, even by our neighbors' standards. My father was a quiet, amiable man and was fondly called Pretty Boy Floyd or Champ by the ladies because of his humorous demeanor. He eventually met and married my stepmother, a Roanoke resident, and unlike my father, I was struggling to find my place.

Figure 2 My free-spirited birth mother, Gladys Campbell.

I knew that I didn't fit in with the other boys in my community because I was gay, although I wasn't familiar with the term then, nor did I know how to come to terms with my identity. I only knew that while felt a connection with them, they didn't have the same connection to me. To escape from this, I would venture downtown to the village, Washington Square Park, or the incredible Central Park. Meeting new people was effortless, and striking up a conversation on a park bench could easily lead to a newfound friendship. The village was an incredible place for anyone who didn't feel like they belonged or weren't accepted in their community. You could always find someone to talk to and feel comfortable around. If you were into rollerblading, it was even better because everyone had their skates on, music blasting

34

from their boomboxes, and could perform tricks. Those weekend excursions were my saving grace, and I felt free. I went exploring around the village, bars which I loved. Stonewall, a gay bar, was interesting, but much more than I was used to at my young age. I also didn't care for the music they played.

I enrolled in a night school in downtown Manhattan to earn the three credits I needed. As I had failed gym, I ended up taking Business Education and completed the course successfully. Afterwards, I decided it was time to pursue college. My stepmother was not unsupportive of this idea, as long as she wasn't required to pay for it. Despite both of my parents having finished high school, my stepmother was not willing to give up her money to support me. Despite always appearing to be broke, she always had money stashed away in her wallet or pinned to her bosom for her personal needs. Whenever I mentioned my plans to attend college, she dismissed the idea quickly and the conversation was over before it had even started.

On my 18th birthday, I reached a breaking point and decided to leave. I had saved up money from working on Fridays and Saturdays at the A&P, carrying groceries for customers. This was back when the A&P was a popular supermarket. I stood outside the store and offered to help people with their groceries, using my cart to transport them. I would carry the groceries all the way to their apartments, even if they were several floors up. Some people were generous and tipped me well, while others only gave me 50 cents or a dollar. Nevertheless, I did this for years to save money for things I wanted, like new sneakers or fashionable clothing.

I had saved $75 by the time I left home, which I gave to my stepmother to hold for me until I had earned a couple hundred more. I also collected beer and Coca-Cola bottles from my neighbors to return for the deposit money. I did whatever odd jobs people would pay me to do. All of this was to save money for my own interests outside of the neighborhood. With my savings, I was able to pay to share an apartment in Greenwich Village with a guy who was studying at NYU.

By attending night school, I graduated high school on time in August 1964, since my birthday is in August. After getting my room, I got a job at the 42nd Street Library, which was the main library in New York City. I attended Hunter College at night while working during the day. However, my job at the library did not pay enough, so I began working with kids at a school called the Lighthouse in New York, which aligned with my major in sociology.

At the Lighthouse For The Blind, I worked parttime as a receptionist. Being there allowed me to work with institutionalized children in group homes. I was able to connect with them because I grew up in a neighborhood where many children came from single-parent families and struggled financially. I observed them going to the armory with their wagons to receive government cheese and other aid, but I never faced those difficulties. Although I had my own room and had everything I needed, there were no extras for surprises. I only had one birthday party celebrating my ninth year, which I forgot to thank my stepmother for, causing her to stop doing anything for my birthday. These experiences made me realize the importance of helping others and the struggles faced by those in my community.

Through my work, I interacted with older people who shared their wisdom and knowledge with me. They often invited me into their homes for a Coca Cola and a chat. These conversations made me realize that staying in my neighborhood was not going to lead to success. I needed to make a change and move downtown, live in my own room, work during the day, and attend school at night. I enjoyed being independent and discovering myself.

At the place where I lived, I had the opportunity to meet a couple of new friends named Lee and Billy. Lee was ex-military and Billy was into computers and from Bethesda, Maryland. Lee hailed from St. Louis. These men provided me comfort as they were the only black guys, who I knew who were gay, that didn't act stereotypically flamboyant. They didn't do anything that I could recall, but they accepted me for who I was. Lee even helped me out by arranging a haircut when my hair grew too long. He was like an older brother who offered guidance when I needed it most, especially since I was living on my own and not running back to my parents' house anymore. Although my stepmother had told me that once I left, there was no going back, it was a terrible situation. She shed crocodile tears when I left, but I knew it was only for show, as everything she did was for my father. She adored him, and I was extra baggage to her. She constantly reminded me of this fact. She made sure I was aware of my status. I accepted that.

First Stop - San Francisco

BREAKING FREE – NY TO CA

Figure 3 Bush and Taylor Street, near my apartment

My lackluster homelife made traveling appealing, I knew that I had to get out of New York. After finishing two years of college by working during the day and attending school at night, I felt I needed another experience. I was reading about Angela Davis and the Freedom Riders and took a bus not knowing exactly where I was going. I boarded a

38

bus to California because I heard that San Francisco and Berkeley were happening places to live.

Among all the places in the United States, California stood out as the ultimate destination for the Hollywood buzz and show business. It seemed like everything I could ever hope to discover was there. Both Berkley and San Francisco had a deliberate liberal mindset, making me feel accepted and allowing me to be myself. I embarked on a bus journey from New York to San Francisco for $99, which took several days to complete. However, upon arrival, I was surprised to find that it was cold in June, as

Figure 4 Downtown from Market Street to Fishermen's Wharf

San Francisco tends to be cooler than other California locations in the summer. I secured a room in a rooming house, but soon realized that San Francisco was not the place for me, especially the downtown Market Street area. There wasn't anything there that truly interested me.

I had heard so much about San Francisco from my time in New York, and it was supposed to be a truly special place. It wasn't like New Jersey, Chicago, Detroit, or any other city. San Francisco had a unique quality all its own, and it wasn't even like Los Angeles. I didn't initially realize that Berkeley was just across the bridge from San Francisco. However, upon arriving, I was disappointed to find that it didn't seem particularly interesting to me; it was just another city. I didn't feel a connection to anything there, and I wasn't aware of Haight Ashbury or Fisherman's Wharf.

As I expressed my dissatisfaction, people started telling me about Berkeley. The manager of the rooming house even suggested that I belonged in Berkley instead of San Francisco. So, I decided to take the bus over to Berkeley and rent a room there.

Berkeley

Then being me, and around the university, I set out to find a job. The idea of working on campus appealed to me. It was my first time seeing a campus with coffee shops and bookstores, and I was in awe. I knew that this was where I needed to be, and I wanted to be accepted by the community there.

Although I wasn't particularly academically gifted and my grades weren't up to Ivy League standards, I discovered that Berkeley had a work-study program for black students. I also became involved with the Black Student Union, where I met educated black students who were not necessarily radical but were very intelligent and often socialized with one another.

One person I met was a black girl named Charlotte, who was studying Russian. I was surprised by her choice of major and wondered why a black girl would study such a language. Being around these higher-level black students gave me a sense of belonging and inspiration.

Even though I wasn't a student at the university, I acted as if I were at the Black Student Union. I ate lunch in the student hall and attended lectures without needing to show any identification.

There was a black man who looked after black students trying to settle in Berkeley and attend the University of California. I was one of those students, and he helped me immensely. I was able to find a job working as an assistant teacher in a progressive elementary school in Berkeley, where my duties included checking papers, helping kids with spelling, and generally assisting the teacher. I did that for about a semester, or no more than a year.

However, I soon realized the potential benefits that Berkeley could offer me. This was the year that Ronald Reagan came to speak at Berkeley, and I was there to witness the protests against him. Even though he was running for governor, he was very controversial. I was proud of the awareness and consciousness of what was happening in the world that I saw around me.

Figure 5 Lake Tahoe weekend trip to gamble and ski

I was given the opportunity to apply for a registered nurse training program at the University of Washington, which had a highly regarded medical school. Unfortunately, my grades were not up to par. They suggested that I enroll in the work-study program at the University of Colorado Boulder to improve my grades. During that summer, I received a stipend, stayed in the dorms, and was among 20 other black students.

As a student in Boulder, I experienced things I had never encountered before, such as hayrides and nightlife at bars. I soon discovered that Boulder, like Berkeley, had a distinct liberal character. Despite this, my grades still needed improvement. I returned to Berkeley and took some classes, even though I was not able to matriculate.

Figure 6 Lake Tahoe weekend trip

During that period, while I was taking classes and attempting to blend in as a student, my primary focus was on survival. My objective was to secure a fulltime job on campus as my efforts to find work in Oakland had been unsuccessful. I acquired a Mo-ped and started working in an office, but it didn't work out. However, I persevered because my yearning was to be a student at Berkeley.

Amidst all the excitement happening with figures like Angela Davis and Stokely Carmichael, as well as other notable events, I longed to be a part of it all. I wanted to engage in conversations and attend various events. There were sign-ups for all sorts of events, petitions to sign, and everything that suited my style at the time.

I had some educated black friends who were all gay. They had a refined demeanor and a wealth of knowledge that I deeply respected. I looked up to them because they were articulate, insightful, and carried themselves with dignity. They didn't care about material possessions or put on airs of luxury; they were just ordinary guys. I also befriended a couple of girls who turned out to be in a same-sex relationship. I felt comfortable around them because they were more intelligent and resourceful than me, and they would guide me to various events and activities. They took me under their wing and made me aware of everything that was available to them as students so I could participate as well.

The Feds Arrived

For two years I worked on campus and immersed myself in the student community. I was living in a house with maybe eight other male students, where we each had our separate rooms. Because Berkeley is a small area, I could and did use my Mo-ped as transportation. I was hanging out, waving to friends, doing this, and doing that when the Feds, FBI, or CIA, came after me, accusing me of being a draft dodger. The agents claimed that I had not notified them every time I moved. I was surprised and insisted that I was not a draft dodger. The agents contacted my parents, who were not aware of my whereabouts other than that I was in California. This was the end of my ideal student life, but my fascination with knowledge goes on.

I freaked out. I was extremely unhappy about being forced to go through a physical examination and being drafted into the military was not something I had ever imagined for myself. I wasn't the type to have strong anti-war beliefs, nor did I want to disclose my sexual orientation and have it follow me for the rest of my life. I discussed my situation with my friends and roommates daily in the week leading up to my departure for induction. I decided to sell everything I had just in case.

During the Christmas break, I attempted to seek help at the university on how to get out of the military before going for induction. However, due to the break, nobody was available to assist me. Fortunately, I was able to find my psychology teacher on campus, who happened to be there. I was almost in tears and asked for his advice. He informed me that he could not diagnose me with any condition that would prevent me from being drafted, but he could write a letter stating that I was the only child in my family attending a university, the only one to carry on the family name, and that I had a nervous condition that caused a speech impediment. It was not a guaranteed solution, but it was worth a try.

On the day of my induction, I went to the Oakland Airbase, where I passed all the necessary exams. The officer told me to get dressed and board the bus, but I questioned him about seeing a doctor. He informed me that I did not need to see a doctor unless I had a reason to do so. I had my letter in hand and was even willing to stand naked to prove my point. Eventually, he asked me to stand aside.

During the induction process, I was apprehensive and nervous. I prayed fervently as I awaited my meeting with the doctor. When I finally met with him, I explained my stance on military service, expressing my love for my country but my unwillingness to fight in a foreign land against people I did not know. I suggested that I would be more suitable for hospital work or other forms of service that would allow me to contribute to my country without compromising my beliefs.

My political consciousness was a driving force behind my stance. I had read that military young black guys were sent to the front lines in Vietnam, and I was troubled by that. I was determined not to be drafted into a war that I did not believe in. While I was careful not to be too confrontational with the doctor, I made it clear that I was a conscientious student who had other ways of serving my country.

The doctor offered a solution and said that he would give a 1Y classification instead of a 4F. This meant that if the situation changed and I felt that I wanted to join the military, I would be accepted. The doctor explained that the 1Y classification was appropriate for me due to my speech impediment, and my nervous condition, made not suitable for frontline combat. I expressed my gratitude and accepted the 1Y classification, which allowed me to leave the building without having to join the military. I quickly got out of that building!

Luxemburg

I thanked God all the way home. Monday morning, I told everybody what happened. Tuesday, I took the bus over the Bay Bridge to San Francisco to a travel agent. I purchased one ticket to New York and the other ticket from New York to Luxemburg. After searching for tickets, we found that the cheapest one was on Icelandic airline. The flight was to Luxemburg. Although I knew nothing about Luxemburg, I remembered hearing people in New York talk about Sweden and how they loved black people there.

I also remembered films with Sammy Davis Jr. who had married a white woman from Scandinavia. Black people were supposed to be a very exotic thing there. Oh, over there, they loved some black. I said, "That's where I need to go." I took the ticket I had to New York to say goodbye to my parents in Queens.

When I revealed the agenda, I caught hell from my stepmother. "What are you going over there for?" "Who do you know over there?" "Don't you be asking for any money?" "Don't you be getting any trouble over there and want us to send you money to come back." "You take your behind over there, you stay over there." "Because we're not sending you money." My stepmother thought I was an idiot and stupid for even thinking about going to Europe. I realized that this was not a great conversation, but I had my own money.

I had dinner with my sweet father, and he told me he had put some money in my pocket. My father and I connected on many levels, but he didn't want to have a problem with his wife. He didn't want to say anything that disagreed with her. He compromised to keep the peace in the house. With what he gave me, I had about $2,500 and a one-way ticket to Luxemburg. After dinner I went to Manhattan to celebrate.

49

I was going to Europe the next day, so I rented a room for a night in Mid-Town Manhattan. It was the weekend, and my plane was leaving on Sunday afternoon. Then I wanted to hit the clubs to celebrate. I called some old friends I had not seen for years to come over and party - to well, a sort of bon voyage party. Friends and people who weren't friends came. We were just drinking and partying.

I invited people back to my room, where we could have some drinks, and the celebration continued. I fell asleep. When I woke up, everyone was gone. In making sure everything was in order and ready for me to go the airport, I discovered I had been robbed. Someone had stolen my money. Luckily, I had somewhere around $150 and my ticket. I know I didn't lose the money. I didn't know what to do. I was in tears. I knew I couldn't go back to my parents. I couldn't call my friends and say I didn't make it. I couldn't go back to California. I was between a rock and a hard place. I was there. What do I do? What would you do?

After praying, I made the decision to go ahead with my travel plans. I was determined to go anywhere the plane would take me. At the airport, I boarded the plane with my one-way ticket to Luxembourg, not really knowing much about the place.

On the plane, I struck up a conversation with a white student who was returning to school in Switzerland. He had just left his family and girlfriend behind. We were around the same age and started talking. He suggested that if he were in my position, he would go to Amsterdam. Although I had heard of Amsterdam, I wasn't familiar with the geography of Europe or the distance between Luxembourg and Amsterdam. Thankfully, sitting next to this guy turned out to be a stroke of good luck as he was a wealth of knowledge.

We arrived at our Luxemburg destination at around 8 or 9 o'clock at night, and to my surprise, there was about three feet of snow on the ground.

I got off with my new friend and went walking in the snow knocking on doors to see if they if we could find a place to stay in the middle of the night, in blowing snow. Looking at the snow blowing past the streetlights, I began to wonder what in the hell I was doing. But we did find a lady who had a room, way upstairs, and almost in the attic. That was a blessing.

The next morning, the guy who was with me had some problems with his traveler's checks, so he had to go to American Express. Before that, he showed me how to buy my train ticket to go to Amsterdam.

Holland / Amsterdam

I arrived by train at the main station in Amsterdam with no idea where to go, I headed for the inquiry desk and asked for help to find a budget friendly place to stay, I was looking for something very cheap like a Youth Hostel. My budget was around $10 a night as all I needed was a bed, a roof over my head, a shower and somewhere to put my clothes.

Staying in a hostel was a great way to meet other travelers who could give me advice on what to see and where to go in the city. If I had stayed in a private place I would have missed out on these valuable connections. In a Hostel there were always around 30 or 40 people from all over the world with different experiences, some of whom had just arrived in Amsterdam and others had been staying there for days or even weeks.

I was relieved to find that the Dutch spoke English very well, I didn't have any problem with the language. Dutch, Swedes, and Danes are known for speaking fluent English, maybe because few travelers speak their languages, so they must communicate in the more widely spoken English.

One night I decided to check out a popular bar that was said to be the "In" place to go. Before I left, I set a goal with myself, which was to network and make connections. Upon arriving 1 ordered a mug of beer, which was all I could afford and scanned the room. I realized that I was one of a few dark-skinned foreigners among a sea of locals.

I always seek out local spots, but I was feeling a little anxious being in a high-end club with such a lack of diversity. As my beer started to run low, I knew I couldn't just stand there without a drink. I moved along the bar and stood near the bartender hoping someone would notice me. Finally, a guy walked up and asked me where I was from, "New York City" I said, he perked up as he had visited New York with his girlfriend. He offered me a drink and invited me to sit with him and his friends, we found we had a lot in common.

I went into my entertainer mode, we discussed New York, and shared jokes and lots of laughter. They asked me to join them, and all go to a late-night club that started around ten thirty. I was declining the offer as the Hostel had a midnight curfew. However, one of them offered me a place to sleep at his house, and I gratefully accepted. We had a great time partying that night, and the next morning I returned to the youth Hostel.

I spent two and a half weeks in Amsterdam, Holland's capital city hoping to find work, but had no luck. I managed to get a job helping someone to move, but quickly realized my language skills were not sufficient for the job market. I was surprised to see many people of Indonesian and African descent; I hadn't realized Holland also had a history of colonialism.

My inability to speak Dutch made it very difficult for me to find work. At the Hostel one morning I met a fellow traveler at breakfast who suggested hitchhiking
through the countryside. He would travel with me some of the way and put me on the right road, the goal being Brussels where it might be easier for me to find work as Belgium was more international. Though I had never hitchhiked before I agreed to join him.

We took a train and got off at some remote location, I was carrying a large Samsonite suitcase and didn't look like a typical hitchhiker. My companion put me on the road to Belgium, and I waited for some time before a car stopped and offered me a ride. The driver could only take me part of the way and dropped me off in a small village. My map reading skills weren't much help in finding my way, it was challenging. At this point I remembered a friend's phone number in Frankfurt and decided to reach out for help. He said come to Frankfurt, you can stay with me for a couple of weeks. I changed my direction and took the road to Frankfurt in Germany.

Scandinavia/Denmark, Sweden, Norway, Finland

Copenhagen: My journey to Copenhagen began with hitchhiking from Germany, without knowing anyone there and only speaking English. To my luck, a businessman driving a Mercedes Benz picked me up and drove me to Denmark. During the ferry ride, we had a meal together, and I was grateful for his company and his fluency in English. Once we arrived in Copenhagen, he dropped me off at the Youth Hostel, where I rented a bed. I found a job at a beer factory that paid well, and with the income, I was able to rent a private room not too far from downtown and work.

Denmark: On New Year's Day in 1968, I arrived in Copenhagen, Denmark, which was to be my first European home. Fortunately, I found a welcoming country that provided me with the necessary support to adapt to a new way of life. Living in Denmark made it easier for me to cope with the challenges of being outside the United States and trying to make a living while becoming a local resident.

I loved my time in Copenhagen so much that I fell in love twice during my stay. I also managed to secure another job there, thanks to a friend, working with kids at an after-school center at the King's Library.

At the invitation of a friend, I attended a Jimi Hendrix concert in Copenhagen despite my unfamiliarity with his music. I was impressed to see the theater filled with young Danes, and I learned that Hendrix was a black musician from Washington State, USA.

My next incredible experience was seeing Josephine Baker perform during one of her farewell tour shows. She was stunning in her attire and sang in both French and English.

During the Easter holiday, I was able to take a week-long, all-inclusive vacation to Palma de Mallorca, Spain, as a tourist. These experiences were truly remarkable and made me feel blessed and highly favored to have them during my first stay in Europe. However, since I had no plans to stay permanently, I began thinking about leaving, even though I was not sure where I would go next. Living in Denmark was amazing, with friendly and approachable locals who spoke some English.

I decided to move to Sweden because I was tired of the press in Denmark, Sweden had a stronger currency, and the people looked better to me. I applied for a Swedish work permit from Denmark.

To save money, I decided to wait for my next big holiday and explore a bit. I took a seven-day boat trip through Scandinavia, visiting Norway, Sweden, Finland, and returning to Denmark. My goal was to find another country with good work potential that I liked. After the trip, I decided to visit Sweden.

We organized outdoor trips for the children where we engaged in music, dance, and rhythm-based activities using various instruments. Our approach was more sound-based, and we emphasized the therapeutic benefits of music. I had obtained my work permit after applying from Denmark, and I believe the institution I applied to was interested in exploring the differences and potential advantages of the American system of childcare.

The institution was known for their experimental and aggressive methods, utilizing progressive types of therapy. Although we didn't employ rhythmic therapy, we recognized the calming effects of music on the children. It was a powerful tool that helped them engage, learn songs, and develop their auditory skills through repetition. Overall, music served as a therapeutic and beneficial tool in our work with the children.

Sweden

Sweden: In Stockholm, I landed a residency job at an institution for children with autism and stayed for a year after obtaining a work permit. I utilized a special treatment for autistic children developed by psychologist Rudolph Steiner. Although Stockholm, Sweden treated me well, I realized after a year that the weather did not suit me as it was too cold. Snowfall was unpredictable, and the winters were harsh. I concluded that

Scandinavia was too cold for me regardless of love or money. Nevertheless, I enjoyed the unique experience of witnessing the June Summer Solstice, where it stays light all day and night in the countryside. These two countries aided my personal growth and self-love, as I interacted with many Danes and experienced the same, if not more, while living and working in Sweden.

Working with autistic children was an unusual experience for me because I don't recall hearing about many kids with autism at that time. I followed Rudolf Steiner's theory of autism and participated in rhythm therapy at an experimental school. The school was situated on private land, consisting of cottages and a large house. I collaborated with the house mother and father, assisting the non-Swedish speaking children. My role was to support them during challenging situations such as when a child began hitting themselves, required assistance with eating, during camping trips or when they experienced temper tantrums.

As I had a couple of days off, I decided to hit the club scene in downtown Stockholm and checked out a popular restaurant. Being in a relationship with both a girlfriend and a boyfriend, I wanted to enjoy both experiences simultaneously. People were enamored with me and wanted to touch my hair and skin, expressing their admiration for my appearance. I often heard, "Oh, I wish I had your color." However, they didn't realize that my looks were the root of the challenges I faced back in America. I chose to leave them to their fantasies.

My work permit was only good for one year and it wasn't being renewed, so I had to search for new job opportunities.

Norway: I had a much smoother journey to Norway compared to my earlier trip to Denmark. Having already decided that I didn't want to stay in Denmark for too long, I took a cruise to Norway through Sweden and enjoyed it a lot. During this time, I received the devastating news of Dr. Martin Luther King's assassination. It hit me hard because he was someone I had met and felt close to. I became disillusioned with my job working with autistic children in Sweden and hoped to start a new chapter of my life.

Finland: I went to Finland when I grew tired of Denmark. I decided to travel to Finland as I didn't intend to live in Denmark permanently. I had some savings, and luckily there was a special package where I could travel from Denmark to Sweden, from Sweden to Norway, and then from Norway to Finland through a series of ships that functioned like a cruise. I thought it was an excellent opportunity to explore the entire Scandinavian region, so I opted for this package.

Finland was very cold, even around Easter. Helsinki, the capital has a large section of the city built underground. The train station and surrounding area are subterranean, a complex of shops, boutiques, cafes, and entertainment. I even had a haircut in an underground barbershop. In cold weather most outdoor life is done underground.

In my time there, the train from Helsinki to St. Petersburg was still running, but for me it was easier to get a train back to Sweden.

Italy: Florence, Tuscany, Milan, Venice, Rome

Florence:
After leaving Sweden I lucked out and was offered a job at a monastery outside the city of Florence. I had been trying every way possible to get to Italy and my prayers were answered.

During the 60's there was a major flood of the Arno River, which washed through the libraries and destroyed many old books and manuscripts. Every day I would take a bus up into the hills to the monastery and set about helping to restore them. Although the job wasn't glamorous and the daily commute up the mountain was tiring, I enjoyed working with the Monks and earning some money. I was shown how to use a heat presser to save the damaged books by applying a thin paper like screen to the pages one by one, the heat from the press would harden them. Unfortunately, many valuable books were too damaged to be saved.

Once there I found a small bed and breakfast guesthouse and discovered Florence. I loved its art museums, art galleries, small winding streets and beautiful buildings. It also has Michelangelo's iconic statue of David.

I left Florence when a cleaning lady unexpectedly opened my room door and found me sleeping with another guy. I had rented it as a single room, so I was asked to leave after breakfast.

I have a vivid memory of enjoying my lunch on a Sunday afternoon in Florence, looking down on the town below. The scene resembled something out of a Charles Dickens novel set during the Christmas holidays. The view was picturesque, with shoppers bustling about on the narrow streets and the sound of church bells ringing in the background. As I sat there, I couldn't help but daydream about what this place must have been like over a hundred years ago, with its small shops and people out for walks and shopping during Christmas.

During the 60s, there was a major flood in Italy that washed away many of the books, and I was tasked with helping to restore them. Every day, I would take a bus up into the mountains where the monastery was located, and they showed me how to use a heated presser to repress the books and a thin paper-like screen to make the paper hard to save them. Unfortunately, some of the books were too damaged to be saved.

All my contacts and people I met told me that I belonged in Milan or Rome where there Is more possibility.

Milan: Living in Milan, Italy was a magical experience, particularly due to the stunning fountains and the unique architectural styles of the buildings. I often had to remind myself that it was all real. One day, a friend introduced me to a woman who had a 15-room penthouse that she let architect students stay. I was grateful for this opportunity, which arose from a friend at the library. My friend at the library had many friends and contacts and through this same connection I was offered a job assisting a professor at the University of Milano.

I felt incredibly blessed that I had landed this job, and I was living on the Via Moscova. I had no idea what I would have done otherwise. Italy was an expensive place to live. I was given an office to read English architectural books featuring different styles of architectural designs. I had to explain what I read to his secretary who spoke English but couldn't understand. The technical English words, so I read, and she translated to Italian for the professor. "We Were a Team", he told us. He was preparing for a conference in California.

Fortunately, my background from New York City, where I had worked at the 42nd St Library and knew about Fashion Week, came in handy. I had always been interested in the Fashion Week event when was held in Bryan Park, Manhattan. And so, I was thrilled to watch the world-renowned designers and beautiful models at Fashion Week in Milan on a sunny afternoon.

I was already overwhelmed with gratitude as I attended the Settimana Della Moda, a semi-annual trade show in Milan. As I was walking around, a man suddenly approached me and asked if I was a model. Trying to answer truthfully without giving away too much, I replied, "I could be." He then offered me a job, stating that my height of 6'3" was perfect for modeling long men's fur coats. I couldn't believe my luck and thanked God profusely. It felt like too much good fortune for someone like me, a tall, slim guy with glasses from the South Bronx, to receive in such a short amount of time. I was sure that God must have been getting tired of my endless gratitude.

Venice:
I remember sitting at a bar in Venice when some military Political News appeared on television. The television stream abruptly cut to darkness, leaving people uncertain about what was going on, the energy around me shifted. I decided to leave Venice the next day, it is important to be aware of the surrounding political climate when traveling. I loved Venice and cherished my time there, all in all I stayed in Italy for a year. Despite this, I loved Venice and cherished my time there.

All in all, I ended up staying in Italy for around a year.

Germany: Berlin, Munich, Dusseldorf

Berlin: Before deciding to live in Germany, I had visited the country several times. During my first visit to Berlin, the city was divided into East and West. I had a frightening experience of almost being stuck in East Berlin while trying to get back to the West. This was a wakeup call for me. I was questioned in a room by Soviet police because I was wearing my fur coat.

Munich: After Berlin, I moved to Munich, a university city located in Bavaria in southern Germany. I chose Munich because it has a rich history and is more liberal compared to some of the northern cities like Frankfurt. People in Munich are also more interested in interacting with foreigners and have more time to socialize.

When I arrived in Munich, I started looking for a job since I had just come from living in Stockholm. The Swedish krona was a strong currency, so I had some mong/flow. I made a lot of contacts while networking in some of the best coffee houses and restaurants in Munich. I also enjoyed people watching on the chic shopping street where I met many interesting people.

I made new connections and frequented some of the best cafes and restaurants of the city. One day, I was buying pastries when I met Edith Schmidt, the owner of the famous club in Munich called "Why Not". The club played soft Rock and Roll not Hard

Rock Jazz. R&B and Motown sounds were very popular in German nightlife. Her club was popular among the wealthy and famous, and she was always looking for unique and diverse talent to work there.

We hit it off, and she offered me a job as a DJ in her club when her current DJ needed time off. Though I didn't have any experience, I expressed my love for music and familiarity with DJs and musicians in New York City. I took the opportunity and started working at Why Not.

To make a long story short, I was not so successful as a DJ. I tried to copy that guy's music. I had his same music platform, that I wrote down; how he started, how the middle and the end came together; and the special songs that he did. I would play most of the songs from the English-speaking realm, and in the R&B realm, or rock and roll.

This was the present guy's kind of rock and roll. I tried to copy his format, but I was not good at mixing. My time was up. When Edith realized that I was not a DJ, instead of telling me I was fired, she made me a host. Munich was becoming more international, she focused on my English speaking as an asset. It was the common language, whether you're French, you're from Japan, or any other country, that wasn't German. Most people did speak English.

She believed I, as the host would make an excellent venue for serving tables and hosting guests. The Why Not was a small yet exclusive club that catered to a select clientele of blueblood entertainers and corporate individuals seeking a leisurely night out. The atmosphere was more focused on good music and socializing rather than dancing, with only invited guests allowed in. The club had a strict entrance policy, with a security guard and peephole screening out those who didn't fit the desired image. This meant that even wealthy Germans and affluent pimps driving Mercedes Benz were denied entry as they did not meet the club's criteria of fame, blueblood status, or corporate affiliation.

I was responsible for seating guests and ensuring their comfort and accommodating any special requests they may have. I often wondered about the patrons always having their own bottle held for them be it Champagne, wine or hard spirits. Guests would purchase their bottle, which would be labelled with their name on a tag and prominently displayed in a cabinet behind the bar if unfinished and held for a future visit. It took me a while to realize it was a common practice in private clubs. Instead of an open tab it was an open bottle, that was a first for me. I was the go-to man, whether it was seating them for privacy or show, dark corners for girlfriends, down-low meetings or in the limelight for others. The tips were very good, and the experience for me was over-the-top. The guests always had a bottle waiting, a constant flow. The club was a symbol of status and exclusivity. Even after consuming half of their bottle, customers could easily order a new one of the same or different brand, which would once again be marked with their name. The ownership of a personal bottle was a symbol of status and exclusivity.

I was employed at that establishment for almost a year when one evening, the management informed me about some English guests coming in, and to be attentive. Although they didn't disclose their identities, I obliged. Soon after, a group of Englishmen, including a black gentleman, arrived in casual attire, and although I recognized them as foreigners, I wasn't sure who they were. That's when I spotted Mick Jagger from the Rolling Stones, among others. I was overwhelmed with excitement but kept my composure.

Mick Jagger, Billy Preston, and Brian Ferry were sitting there in regular clothes, drinking, and socializing. Although I wasn't directly serving them, I was apprehensive about summoning the waitresses to tend to their needs. Instead, I circulated around the tables, ensuring everyone was comfortable, everything was in order, and the waitstaff was performing their duties adequately. I was especially keen on taking care of our special guests, despite feeling quite nervous.

"Why Not" only stayed open from eight to 11 p.m. at night. By midnight, it was over, but people still wanted to party. There was another disco club called Josephine's, and they asked me to escort them there. I went with them in a Mercedes-Benz 600 limousine to Josephine's. When we arrived, we entered through the security entrance, and were taken to a private table upstairs in the VIP section. This was one of the highlights of my Munich stay.

I danced with Joan Baez in Munich. The party began once she took off her shoes. I still have vivid memories of dancing with Joan Baez.

Munich held a special place in my heart as it reciprocated my affection. It was a delight to have a cozy apartment of my own and a friendly neighbor next door to hang out with. Our mornings were filled with coffee and pleasant conversations, while our afternoons and evenings were laced with a touch of hash. Unfortunately, the economy took a turn for the worse, and as a foreigner, it became increasingly difficult for me to find work. The situation deteriorated rapidly, and people began to withdraw from social activities. In search of a better alternative, I turned to friends who suggested that Dusseldorf might be the next best option for me to stay in Germany.

Düsseldorf: Dusseldorf, a vibrant and prosperous city known for its numerous banks and large factories, welcomed me with open arms. Taking the train to this new city, I landed a job at a club thanks to my prior experience at Why Not. The old part of the city, Altstadt, was a charming area with cobblestone streets and remarkable architecture. The lively atmosphere created by the clubs, and bars made it a festive spot. Although I was employed at a club in this area, the hours were scarce due to a lack of patrons. I persisted for some time, but unfortunately, I couldn't extend my work permit, which meant I couldn't stay in Germany either. I was unemployed for some time until I received a job offer working under the table at a private gay club, which I accepted out of necessity.

Although I wasn't the best bartender, my service skills and focus were enough for the smaller bar. Working at this club proved to be a unique and eye-opening experience. I even met someone there who invited me out for my birthday, which I gladly accepted. After dinner, we headed to Rock & Roll bar that had a hip pool hall vibe with long-haired, artsy patrons. It was a fun happening place. I couldn't have asked for a better way to celebrate my birthday in a local hangout bar.

My friend, who seemed to have connections in the industry, introduced me to a friend of his, who was brilliant and spoke several languages, including English, French, and German. He was into photography and loved taking people's photos. We hit it off because of our shared interest in jazz, blues, rock and roll, and R&B. Although I didn't know many people in the area, I enjoyed spending time with him, he was well-versed in many subjects. Over time, we became great friends, and we remain close to this day, even after 45 years. Thanks to our friendship, I have visited Israel 12 times, including my first trip in 1975.

That sums up my experience in Munich and Dusseldorf. Despite my limited German language skills, I tried to maintain some fluency to reflect my two years of living in Germany - one year in Munich and one year in Dusseldorf.

Upon returning to New York, my home base, I looked for a job in my field. With my degree in sociology and a minor in special education, I found a job in childcare. My previous experience working with kids in Sweden and Denmark served me well, as I worked with neglected and deprived children who were wards of the court in New York State institutions. Later, I worked as a supervisor in group homes, thanks to my educational background and work experience.

Romania

Figure 7 Creative art made with hay from the fields Farm for art sculpture.

My next trip to Europe was a trip to Romania. The best way to get to Cluj-Napoca is to fly to Budapest and take the train to Cluj. At the Hungarian/Romanian border the train is boarded, guards check the passengers' passports then the train continues.

I had several days in Budapest sightseeing. The short river boat cruise takes you down the Danube between the two ancient cities, Buda on one side and Pest on the other. The night life was wild and fun, the people interesting and the history of the area very chaotic.

Cluj is one of the best university towns in Romania, famous for several specialist Medical Colleges. The nightlife is more cafe than club, yet the students study hard.

Skiing is very popular in the winter; summertime is rolling hills and picturesque country villages. I was traveling through the country in a camper with friends when we stopped in a valley with a gypsy encampment. We were invited to join them for the evening, it was such a breathtaking experience dancing to Gypsy music, singing around an outdoor fire and passing around a jug of wine. We enjoyed ourselves until dawn, my unforgettable Romanian memory.

I later learned that Romania is home to a church for each day of the year, and that Transylvania is where the real Dracula Castle and fortress can be found.

Calvin Campbell

Figure 8 Liked the grandfather and child selling flowers.

Figure 9 A church and the grounds - nicely done.

Israel

In Israel, I experienced a profound sense of awe as I mingled with people from all over the world in places like the Dead Sea, Jerusalem, and the Wailing Wall. Drinking from Jacob's Well in Samaria was an unforgettable moment for me.

I love Israel and I've been there many times. Tel Aviv has beautiful beaches and lovely waterfront dining. During that time, it had a good night life located at some amazing outdoor sites.

Sometimes we would drive to Jerusalem from Tel Aviv to visit the old city and the Wailing Wall. I put my written prayer between the stones within the wall and I walked the path where Christ carried his cross. We also had fun visiting the stadium near the Jaffa Gate, where concerts were held. We sat on the hill within hearing distance. My friends loved American jazz and R & B, favoring saxophones.

Sometimes we would stay overnight at a kibbutz, or sometimes we would only have lunch. A kibbutz is a collective agricultural settlement. It was a harsh environment. The Sea of Galilee is swampy, the Judean mountains are rocky, and south of the country, the Negev, is mostly desert.

Tel Aviv was very different, it has everything. The outdoor markets in South Tel Aviv near Jaffa have interesting river front shopping malls with high quality products and interesting people. During my stay, I saw the international singer Gloria Gaynor known for her hits "I WILL SURVIVE" and - "I AM WHAT I AM". She was speaking how I felt. She was singing to me personally.

My main reason to visit Israel so many times is because I support the Jewish state and because they are progressive. Israel is one of the few places in the world where being gay or female are not looked down on. I always felt safe walking in Tel Aviv at night. In addition, they are culturally inclusive. It is not uncommon to see people from Ghana, Ukraine, Ethiopia, Russia, and other places looking for a better life. If you are Jewish from anywhere in the world, you may live in Israel.

I enjoyed sightseeing in Jaffa and Heron eating fish with my Palestinian cousins in their part of the city. On almost every trip, I made sure that I spent time in their area down by the port.

As outsiders to their neighborhood, my friend and I did have some unfortunate experiences with young kids throwing stones at the car.

I love Caesarea, an ancient port city built by the Romans with the famous aqueducts. An aqueduct is a water-carrying bridge that runs above the ground and transfers water from rivers to dry areas, like a hose. The aqueduct was built about 2000 years ago during the reign of Harold and is no longer in use except for visiting tourist buses.

Cyprus (North / South)

I lived in Northern Cyprus for two years before moving to Egypt for one year.

Cyprus is very ancient, having been settled by first Greeks then Romans. There are many ancient ruins all over the island. The island split in 1974, when Turkey invaded to support Turkish Cypriots in response to a military coup which was backed by the Athens government. This

resulted in the Greeks controlling the South and the North being controlled by Turkey. Cyprus is a fascinating Island, the North with the world-famous fun resort city Kyrenia, now called Girne by the Turks, and Nicosia, the last divided city in Europe. The city has a wall built right through the center, with soldiers guarding the few gates for people to pass from one side to the other, but you need permits from both sides to do so. Cyprus is extremely popular as a vacation spot for people from Europe and

Israel. There are excellent boats to Turkey, Greece, and Israel from both North and South Cypress.

Figure 10 Renovated historic building used as marketplace.

Figure 11 Saint Hilarion Castle in Kyrenia, North Cyprus

Figure 12 Sight-seeing in Northern Cyprus

Russia

It was very important to learn more about African blood in Russia. Alexander Pushkin, the poet, playwright, novelist born of a Russian woman and an Angolan man who was born in Uzbekistan. The Angolan descended from an African slave father.

St Petersburg: I took the Red Arrow from Moscow to St. Peterburg. I have now been in both "St. Petersburgs". I visited the one in Russia and I live in the one in Florida. St. Petersburg Russia is one of the most beautiful cities in Europe.

The Red Arrow, famous for its history, is a wonderful, elegant train, mostly wood with sleeper cabins and white glove service. It leaves St. Petersburg Station at

Figure 13 Alexander Puskin statue

79

five minutes to midnight. The trip takes eight hours between cities.

Moscow: Moscow is the capital and largest city of Russia. The city stands on the Moskva River in Central Russia, with a population estimated at 13.0 million residents within the city limits, over 17 million residents in the urban area, and over 21.5 million residents in the metropolitan area.

Calvin Campbell

Figure 14 Red Square in Moscow

Figure 15 The museum Hermitage in Moscow

Figure 17 *St Petersburg Russia museum*

Figure 16 *"McDonalds and they are delicious" in Moscow*

Africa - Southern

Mozambique: My love and curiosity for Africa led me onto Mozambique, on the southeast coast of Africa, which has a vibrant culture of both Arabs and Africans. A civil war had just been resolved and as my plane landed, I found myself a little worried about any lingering strife.

Maputo the capital (now the main port city) used to be called Lourenco until 1976. It was originally built by the Portuguese as a fort on the estuary of Delagoa Bay on the Indian Ocean and became the capital of Portuguese colonial East Africa. The Portuguese influence showed throughout the city, the white buildings with flags flying reminded me of Lisbon, and people were friendly. I had a good time exploring the city and happily found all my concerns unfounded.

Ivory Coast: I had planned to visit Accra, Ghana, but I stopped in the French speaking Ivory Coast since it was close by. However, I encountered a problem when I arrived because my travel guidebook, which was outdated, stated that I did not need a visa to enter the country, but I found out that I did. The police were respectful and took me to their office to sort out the issue.

I explained that I was planning to go to Ghana after the Ivory Coast and that I had already booked a business class hotel in Abidjan, the largest city in the Ivory Coast. However, since it was late at night, the police couldn't process the matter until Monday. Once everything was clarified, the police escorted me to my hotel, which was very kind of them since the tourist buses had already left, and the taxi drivers spoke French, which I didn't understand. I offered the police something to drink as a token of appreciation.

After the police left, I was relieved that the situation had been resolved, but I still needed to figure out how to obtain a visa to stay in Abidjan. Despite the kindness of the police department, a visa was still necessary. I spoke with the hotel concierge, who was aware of my situation and offered to help. The next day, a young tourist guide from the airport, came to the hotel and accompanied me to the airport police station where he vouched for me as his guest. I was then granted a visa. I felt fortunate that I was staying at a high-end hotel that provided such assistance, which turned a stranger into a friend and guide. He showed me around his neighborhood and even took me to his house to meet his children. The people I encountered were incredibly courteous and helpful, which was a blessing because the situation could have turned out differently if not for their generosity.

Later, I discovered that I also needed a visa to enter Ghana, which I hadn't realized before. Again, he accompanied me to the

Ghanaian embassy to inquire about obtaining a visa to enter Ghana after leaving the Ivory Coast.

While at the Ghanaian embassy, I filled out the visa application form. However, it was during the Christmas holiday season and things were moving slowly. I expressed my eagerness to visit my friends in Ghana to the processor but was informed that it would take a few days for the application to be processed and returned to me. When I returned a few days later, the application was still pending. I was advised to return before New Year's Eve, which I did. I was given a tourist visa and ended up staying a week. Abidjan is called the Paris of West Africa. I still have friends there to this day.

Egypt

My first sight of the Pyramids of Giza was breathtaking and the age of them amazed me. Then being allowed to go inside and up close was an out of this world experience. The famous Cairo Museum filled with artefacts of that ancient civilization was worth negotiating the heat and chaos of Cairo itself. I stayed in Luxor as my base and explored Egypt for a year, then I went to see the Valley of the Kings and on to Aswan. There I became friends with the local Nubian people who had lived on that area of the Nile for thousands of years. I stayed with the Nubians for a month, and then went back to Cypress.

* Sharm El Sheikh which is a Diplomatic center and tourist hub
* Dahab with exceptional restaurants on the waterfront, there big on Windsurfing and Desert trips and popular

Figure 18 Exploring Giza and the pyramids.

The Temple of Karnak in Luxor – which was Egypt's old imperial capital called Thebes. It is the largest in Egypt. There were no libraries in ancient Thebes, so history was recorded on the walls in Hylogrifities.

ure 19 Bedouin Nomads in Egypt

Figure 21 Riding a camel in Egypt

Figure 20 Celebrating with gratitude for a friend's new home.

Figure 22 Valley of the Kings in Luxor Egypt where I lived for a year.

Turkey

Figure 23 Turkey where I had my clothing line manufactured.

I have been to Turkey several times, and even spent a year enjoying my life in Izmir. Then I started my manufacturing business making men's suits. The city if Izmir is on the beautiful Aegean Sea, with access by ferry to the port of Thessaloniki in Macedonia. The trip takes around fourteen hours. Meanwhile a short trip by ferry from Izmir takes you across the bay to Karsiyaka, an historical cultural city that has a direct road to Istanbul. Sometimes Istanbul is called the doorstep to Europe. Built on the ruins of Constantinople, it's fascinating history holds so many challenges. The Romans, the Greeks and then the Ottoman Empire all jumbled together, from the beautiful Byzantine church of St. Sophia, which is now a museum. The famous Blue Mosque and the ancient Roman cisterns built to supply water to the city, now repaired with original Greek and Roman artifacts. Traveling through Turkey I found everyone was proud of Ataturk, he brought Turkey into the modern world.

Calvin Campbell

Florida

South Beach: After leaving Germany, I returned to the U.S. I wanted to go to San Francisco where I had friends but was offered a job in New York. The AIDS epidemic and recession were equally bad in both places, so I wasn't thrilled with either choice. Then friends who had left New York for Florida said come to South Beach, so I packed up and left New York behind. Fortunately, I easily found an apartment and reconnected with my New York friends.

One of my friends was a Turkish tailor who I had bought suits from in New York. He had been urging me to visit him in Turkey and had just now moved his family to the States. When I arrived in South Beach, he and his family were in the process of opening a club called Zen.

Calvin Campbell

In Figure 24 Club hopping in South Beach in a limo – Party days.

South Beach, I faced some opposition when I shared my idea of opening a small skincare clinic with my associates at Zen. They pointed out that I was new in town and didn't know anyone and suggested that I work with them instead. Since I already had a job, we agreed that I would help with the decorations and preparations, and in return, they would give me VIP status. Everything was set for the grand opening on New Year's, but just before that, my friends in New York invited me to work at Saks for Christmas and earn some extra money. I could still make it back to Zen for the opening, so I agreed and stayed at my friend's house in Brooklyn.

93

At Saks Fifth Avenue, I quickly proved myself to be skilled and in demand at the store. Two French brothers, and their father owned a pharmaceutical company called Santa Fe. They helped to introduce the new fragrance called Hanae Mori, named after a Japanese designer of Couture from Paris. It was very successful, and SAKS put the fragrance in the case with such brands as Chanel, Christian Dior, and Prada. Business was going so well, and we were so busy, SAKS gave us a second location in the store. They had initially hired someone to promote their product, but he had made mistakes that damaged their reputation. Since they were going back to France for the holidays, they needed someone to watch over their new product line, and everyone recommended me. I liked the fragrance and accepted the job.

I did well and sold a lot of fragrances, which earned me promises of future stores. When I returned to South Beach for Zen's opening night, I was the VIP host and made a lot of money from tips for three months. However, the owner eventually said they couldn't pay me as much and offered the club for a night to host my own parties instead. After considering the offer, I took Sunday as my night to host parties.

I consulted with my spiritually inclined friends, who were into yoga, reflexology, tarot cards, and healing, and we decided to host a party called the Trans Zen Dance Celebration. Instead of guests coming through the front door, we directed them through an alleyway, adorned with tiki lamps, red carpet, and velvet ropes.

Once they entered, we guided them to the front and back of Stage Two, then to the red room, where we held a drum circle.

Many women who left the beach at five o'clock did not want to go home and preferred to shop or stay out as long as possible before having to work on Monday. They returned on Sunday nights and paid $10 to get into my smoke-free venue. They enjoyed the neutral environment, free from the unwanted advances of men. While we initially attracted mostly women, men eventually started showing up as well.

The club's drum circle on Wednesdays attracted crowds of 300 or more people. My parties were held on Sundays from five to eleven p.m. and featured different themes such as Middle Eastern, Jamaican, and African. I also created product-focused themes where specialists would move around the room featuring their products, such as reflexology or body massages in different sections.

My events received write-ups in the Miami Herald. These articles provided proof of my success. Three months later, the Hanae Mori guys called me and said they had some stores in Miami.

South Beach, Florida. It was the only place I was familiar with in Florida. However, I knew that South Beach was not the same as the rest of Florida. I considered Fort Lauderdale since I used to go there with my white friends during spring break when I was in college. I enjoyed partying there, but South Beach resonated with me more. I decided to move to South Beach and look for a place to live. Additionally, I wanted to visit the Dominican Republic and Puerto Rico because I found them intriguing. I started my trip to South Beach in May and a few days later, I traveled to the Dominican Republic where I spent a week before going to Puerto Rico. Finally, I returned to South Beach.

While South Beach was always pleasant, it didn't seem like the ideal place for me to live at the time. On the other hand, I found San Juan in Puerto Rico more appealing. However, it was in

Figure 25 Sunday afternoon beach party

South Beach where I met Larry from Virginia, and we instantly bonded over our shared Virginian roots. Larry was known as the black interior decorator for all the clubs, and he was the go-to person for clubs when they wanted to have special events. His ability to get into any club made him a valuable connection for me. Whenever I wanted to attend a party, I would hang out with Larry. I was impressed by the way he lived and presumed he was making good money. His reputation and prestige made me even more interested in returning to South Beach. Now, I had an "in" and a valuable connection. Larry and some of his acquaintances moved to South Beach, and I used the money my father left me to purchase a condo. My parents had always stressed the importance of having a place of your own where no one could tell you to leave, and that's precisely what I have now.

Initially, I was cautious about renting in a predominantly white neighborhood, so I made sure my neighbors were okay with me being there. After renting for a year, the landlord offered to sell the property, but I always prioritize getting a good sense of the neighborhood before buying anywhere. Fortunately, I was once again lucky in South Beach.

I was successful in my work because I was determined and well-liked. I had no tolerance for those who didn't sell my merchandise, but those who did were my friends. Eventually, my territory grew, and I was given more stores to manage, such as

Neiman Marcus and Bloomingdale's in Atlanta, and Charleston in South Carolina. I also had a store in Birmingham, Alabama.

Figure 26 Conducting a training as the National Trainer for Hanae Mori in Miami Beach FL

Once again, I was blessed with a stroke of luck. One Sunday, I decided to visit the Bal Harbour store to check on the arrangement of my product cases and speak with the weekend staff to ensure they were pushing my product. Although I was mostly in the back case, I wanted to make sure everything was going smoothly. After checking on things, I decided to take a coffee break upstairs. Since it was Sunday, I didn't have much work to do, and no one was working my case.

As I was going up the escalator, I noticed a lady smiling at me and giving me a wave. She was a black lady who had on a big hat and sunglasses, accompanied by two other ladies. I immediately thought she was likely one of my customers. Given that we were at Bal Harbour, where Saks and Neiman were located, there were not many black customers. I had seen this before and knew the routine. I went back down to the store and heard someone say, "Do you know who that was? "It was Oprah Winfrey!", someone said. I couldn't believe it. I thought, "I knew I wanted her to be my customer."

I had heard that Oprah occasionally visited Bal Harbour on Sundays. Without hesitation, I dashed down the stairs, as the escalator was too slow, and grabbed from my supplies - perfumes, body products, and a basket to put it all in. As the national trainer in the Southern Region, I filled the basket, shrink-wrapped it, tied a bow, and added my business card to it. I then presented the basket to Oprah, simply stating that it was a gift because of who she is. She graciously accepted it and even let me spray it on her, which I enjoyed. I didn't do it for a photo op, and I was grateful for the opportunity to meet her.

The following week, everyone seemed to know about my encounter with Oprah. I constantly heard comments like "Oh, you met Oprah!" and "I heard you met Oprah, Oprah, Oprah, Oprah." However, after weeks went by, the staff started to question why I hadn't received a thank you from Oprah, not even from her friend Gail. The began saying "That's not like Oprah." "It was hard to believe after all the high-end products she received as a gift." I never received any form of acknowledgement from her.

In November, Nordstroms in Chicago on Michigan Avenue began receiving inquiries about the "Oprah fragrance." Neiman Marcus denied having any fragrance named after Oprah and was unaware of the name. However, they didn't carry any fragrance by Oprah, and people continued to call. Eventually, they discovered that the fragrance was named "Butterfly" or "Hannah," When Oprah mentioned it on her Christmas show in November, the store moved it from the back case and displayed it in the case beside Chanel and Dior. The fragrance became incredibly popular, and my company took off. It was a blessing that it happened to me. I felt blessed and was grateful.

I would go out on Saturday nights, and people would recognize me because of my success with the Oprah fragrance. I became a regular at all the clubs and was able to get in without any trouble. People knew who I was and what I represented, and I became the big cheese in South Beach.

It took Hanae Mori (FYI: Japanese designer who made the fragrance) years to release another fragrance, but it didn't match up to the quality of their earlier fragrances. Despite this, I remained loyal to them for fifteen years. In retail, your past accomplishments don't matter - it's all about meeting current sales targets and exceeding previous year's numbers.

Eventually, I decided to quit and move on. They suggested I stay on part-time, but I knew that in retail, there's no such thing as part-time during the holiday season. So, I left and traveled to Costa Rica and then to the Dominican Republic, where I purchased a timeshare property in Puerto Plates in the Dominican Republic.

Central America: Costa Rica, Dominican Republic, Cuba, Jamaica

Costa Rica: Having lived in Miami and South Beach for 15 years, in 2008 during the Great Recession, I decided to leave the United States once again. After working as National Trainer and Southeast Regional for Hanae Mori perfumes I decided to say Adios and left for Costa Rica. I passed through San Jose, the capital and made my way to Limon, a working-class city of mostly black residents. It is a busy main port, a little festive, a little shady, and a little shabby. But still as expensive to live as San Jose.

When considering living in a foreign place, it's important to think about the exchange rate and the value of your money. Sometimes you get more bang for your buck, but other times it's almost even. Unfortunately, in Costa Rica, things were twice as expensive as I had imagined. I had heard that Puerto Viejo was a tourist paradise. I stayed in a nightclub area with plenty of bars which was great for partying.

Calvin Campbell

103

However, it was challenging to find affordable housing to buy. All the nice properties with white sand beaches were owned by foreigners. The only beach front house I could afford had no electricity and black sand; the cables were already laid in the area but had to be connected. Although Puerto Viejo, Costa Rica was a fun place to party, it wasn't the right fit for me to live permanently. I moved on to the Dominican Republic.

Dominican Republic: Moving around the Dominican Republic there was a beautiful beach near Santa Domingo airport called Boca Chica. The town was very interesting, with many timeshares and casinos that exuded a Caribbean flair. The people there were extremely welcoming, and I stayed in a hotel that allowed me to attend their parties at night.

During my stay, I was introduced to the concept of timeshares, and there was a beautiful and charming girl who tried to convince me of their benefits. She explained that not only could I use the timeshare in the Dominican Republic, but also at any other locations around the world since they were part of a larger chain. I thought it was a great idea since it would provide me with a consistent level of quality when traveling. In the end, I decided to sign up for the timeshare program.

On my subsequent visits to the Dominican Republic, I stayed in the city of Santo Domingo, which was a magnificent town with friendly people and nice side streets. The city had a black tone to it in terms of race, but there was no oppression and a liberal mentality prevailed. The nightlife was lively, and there were many places to enjoy entertainment and art.

I visited the city three or four times because it was always cheap to travel from Miami, and I enjoyed the party atmosphere and learned new salsa and merengue steps. I highly recommend putting the Dominican Republic on your travel list.

If you enjoy going out in the evenings and socializing, Santo Domingo has a Walking Street, also known as the Promenade, where you can walk from one end of the boulevard to the other. It's like an outdoor market, with shops, coffee shops with outdoor seating, and people playing music and doing acrobatics. The city has a natural charm about it, and the people are good-looking. Overall, I give Santo Domingo a thumbs up and recommend it as a travel destination.

It's just a cool place to go because you're in the Caribbean, and there are people of color.

Although I wouldn't consider it unsafe, I would advise caution and moderation when it comes to drinking. Personally, I've never had any issues, but I believe it ultimately comes down to how you conduct yourself and the choices you make. As long as you're responsible and act normally, you should be fine.

On a separate note, there's another place I enjoy visiting, although I've only been there twice - Puerto Rico. During my last trip, I spent a weekend in San Juan before heading to San Jose. While I had hoped to visit Ponce, something came up and I wasn't able to make it. However, I thoroughly enjoyed exploring El San Juan with its beautiful architecture and Spanish cobblestone streets. The beachfront hotels were also quite lovely.

Unfortunately, I'm not sure what the current state of Puerto Rico is following the recent hurricanes. Nonetheless, Puerto Ricans are some of my favorite people with whom I feel a strong kinship due to being a New Yorker and sharing that connection with many Puerto Ricans.

Moving on to the Dominican Republic, there is a beautiful beach near Santa Domingo airport called Boca Chica. It's the perfect party spot, with palm trees, food service, and even the opportunity to rent a room. I used to take a taxi from my place in the Old City to get there, and my friend would sometimes drive me. It's close to the airport and a little slice of paradise, where I even had monkeys come sit on my shoulder. I can't believe I forgot to include it in my story about the Dominican Republic! But trust me, Boca Chica is a must-visit spot.

Cuba: Their ancestry is a fusion of indigenous Indian and Afro, mainly Indian, resulting in a light brown complexion. Some may mistakenly assume they have a mixed black and white background, but it's actually a blend of black and Indian heritage. The diversity of appearances and characteristics that arise from combining various cultures fascinates me. During my travels, especially in Central and South America, I'm amazed by the mixtures and unique beauty that exist, making me appreciate my

Figure 27 Fortress in Havana - Historic Cuba symbol

own mixed ancestry even more. It's a gift to recognize and embrace our identity as a blend of African American, African, Brazilian, Afro Cuban, and Afro Columbian.

I embarked on an adventurous journey to Havana, Cuba, via a Jamaican Airlines flight. The trip allowed me to witness the everyday life of the Cuban people and gain a greater appreciation for my own freedom and life's blessings. Despite a power outage during a night of partying in an underground club with locals, I felt grateful for the experience.

As the United States had placed an embargo on Cuba, Jamaicans were still permitted to travel to Cuba. Despite my uncertainty about the exact location of my destination, my faith guided me through the journey, and I was determined to enjoy my trip to the fullest while avoiding any legal trouble due to my presence in Cuba.

While traveling, I encountered a German man who advised me to have a specific address in Havana ready for my stay. He cautioned me against arriving in Cuba without an address and searching for accommodation upon arrival. He recommended that I use the address of the boarding house where he was staying, and I heeded his advice. During my trip, the Cuban government did not stamp my American passport; instead, they provided me with a stamped piece of paper as evidence of my legal entry into Havana. I also carried a visa indicating my date of entry, which did not cause any issues during my travels. When I returned to Jamaica, I was instructed to discard the stamped paper.

Figure 28 Cuban history museum

My experience in Havana was quite intriguing. The architectural style of the 1950s was fascinating, but unfortunately, there was a great deal of damage to the buildings that required restoration. I visited several museums, and, despite the communist regime, I listened to their account of Castro's history. I am not inclined towards politics, and my primary purpose was to admire the relics in the museums. However, most of my time was spent observing people as they went about their daily routines. It was common to see residents selling goods from their apartment windows, particularly those living on the ground floor. The bustling street scene was filled with vendors selling all kinds of items.

Upon entering the mall, I noticed locals sitting in the coffee shop located on the lower level. Curious, I decided to head upstairs to explore the offerings of the many stores in case I wanted to make any purchases. However, upon reaching the upper level, I found that most stores were empty and devoid of customers. The sparsity of available merchandise for sale was very noticeable, especially considering it was a mall. It looked like the last day of a going out or business sale. It looked like the last day of a "going out of business sale."

In Havana I stayed with a Russian widow who had been married to a Cuban military man. She had a bed and breakfast, a large house with six rooms to accommodate guests, and a maid to prepare breakfast.

After breakfast, I took a taxi to downtown. Since the residence was situated a little outside the city center. At times, I had to share the taxi with four or five other passengers who were also headed into the city. If I chose to take the bus, the lines and waiting times were long, which was not a good option. Overall, transportation in Havana was not the most efficient or convenient.

I looked at a lot of churches and parks where they had one. My favorite was the Malacon. People walked to promenade along the San Cristobal church area, where there were several very popular outdoor cafes. A famous place to meet and be seen.

In the old part of Havana, there are cafes and restaurants, geared towards tourists. Here is where we would find small roving bands with maybe a singer, a drummer, a guitar player, and a bongo player that play in the restaurant for about 10 or 15 minutes. They get the spirit going, pass the hat, and go to the next one. All right now. It lifted your spirits when you're alone in a restaurant and you don't know anyone. All of a sudden, the band comes in and starts singing and playing music. It would change the atmosphere of the rest restaurant.

One time I even went to the beach, which is outside the city. To get there, you go through a low tunnel and on the other side there's another suburban-like area. This is where the beach and everything looks almost like time stood still. There are hotels outside the city, but it was hard to tell if they were occupied. The beach littered with old equipment and little umbrellas. To enjoy the experience, you must overlook those things, the destruction, and other local issues the country was in the midst of. You cannot be political. You want to be thankful thar you can interact with the Cuban people.

I never talked about politics, but I embraced the people. They are our brothers and sisters. I felt bad for them. I tried to enjoy them for the moment for the time that I was there. I even went to a club there.

Someone informed me about their club's location and provided me with tickets for the night. The club was situated in a basement, or perhaps more accurately, in a cellar. Despite its subterranean location, it was a spacious venue, accommodating up to 150 individuals who were all enjoying themselves by dancing and indulging in drinks. However, when the lights suddenly went out, some remained in the basement while most stepped outside to escape the heat and waited on the sidewalk for the lights to come back on, if they ever did. I personally stayed there for approximately a week and a half, thoroughly relishing the experience, and making acquaintances along the way.

Although my Spanish skills were not top-notch, I still managed to meet people and explore the city on foot, as it was known to be a great walking city. Downtown was bustling, and transportation options included, shared taxis (squeezing in maybe four or five people), or minibuses that stopped frequently to pick up passengers. While I often opted for a taxicab on my return trip after a long day of sightseeing, I still enjoyed the lively atmosphere of Havana and even ventured out at night to explore various neighborhoods. While strolling around, I peeked into windows to catch glimpses of people's daily lives, looking to see if they had televisions and what kind of lighting inside their apartments. I did so discreetly to avoid drawing unwanted attention from the police who occasionally cast a suspicious glance in my direction. Despite this, I felt safe and was never approached by anyone. My main aim was to observe the locals' social lives and I visited some cafes in the evening to do so. The atmosphere was lively with people laughing and having a good time, regardless of their economic status. While the economic system in Havana made life challenging for many, I still found the city enjoyable and fascinating to visit.

Nicaragua

Managua: I wanted to leave the United States around 2007 or 2008, but I didn't know where to go. Since I was looking for a second residency to operate a business, I decided to go to Nicaragua, which is in Central America with a Caribbean flavor. I stayed in Managua, the capital, but unfortunately, there was not much going on since there was no central area. Nicaragua has had issues with, volcanoes, mismanagement, and infrastructure construction. Although it doesn't show, many other Central and South American countries, particularly in the capital cities, look better.

I stayed in a hostel, which is another name for a rooming house. Everyone had bars on their doors, and there were gates where you could sit outside like a balcony or front porch, but you were gated inside. People could talk to you through the bars, but they couldn't come in. Local grocery stores had bars, and the attendants gave you the products through them. As a foreigner, I didn't like all that. I stayed in Managua for too long and decided to leave for a place I had heard about called Bluefield, which is on the Caribbean side.

Bluefield: In Bluefield, there are mixed-colored people who have flavor and are not trying to be white. I stayed in a hotel owned by a black family. The wife had passed away, and the husband was trying to carry on. I met many of the people who lived around there or worked for the hotel. Many of them spoke English, and we became friends. Although my Spanish was not that great, I knew some words, and some of them knew English words.

Bluefield had a pleasant atmosphere and attractive residences. Exploring the local parks at night was a delightful experience, but I yearned for more. By conducting proper research and exercising due diligence, one can discover that the Caribbean side is generally populated by people of color. Personally, I preferred staying on the Caribbean side, but my time spent in Bluefield was comfortable and charming. Despite my fondness for the area, I only stayed there for a couple of days.

Corn Island: I heard about Corn Island, which was reported to have a significant black population. The mayor and the school superintendent were both black, and the educated black middle class of Nicaragua resided there, living in comfortable homes with well-manicured lawns. Many black people owned fish container businesses for storing fish before exportation. The hotels were also owned by black people, and I was impressed by the prosperity of the middle-class black community in Nicaragua. It was an eye-opener for me because these individuals were relatively unknown despite their success.

They also have indigenous Indians there, but many Indians arrive there and become squatters. They weren't having that. They would burn them out. Then the problem was not because they were indigenous. There were indigenous people who lived there for a generation. The problem was with newcomers who migrate to a place to find work. Then they squat, but that peaceful setting and Corn Island was not having it.

The homes in Bluefield and Corn Island are breathtaking, with some dating back to the 1800s and meticulously maintained. These places get a thumbs up from me anytime the conversation turns to people of color, not just for their safety. Although Corn Island is a popular tourist destination, I like it because it is a melting pot where tourists mingle with locals who live comfortably.

I appreciate the government's effort to maintain the public areas and ensure everything looks good. There's a small mall where people can shop and dine at restaurants. I was thrilled to see people enjoying themselves and expressing their pride in being Black. These places are where you strike gold, leaving behind the likes of Managua and exploring Bluefield, Corn Island, and beyond. That's my story.

Venezuela: My next destination was Venezuela, where I was fascinated by the intelligence and culture. I landed at Caracas airport and then took a bus to Maracaibo, a resort area located in Allegro. From the bus station, you board a small bus that wind up a mountain that's usually just a single lane. Only one car can pass at a time, so you have to stop and let the other vehicles pass before you can continue. The traffic goes up the cliff, and then the bus goes around and around to come down the other side. If you're daring enough to look down, you pray that the driver is neither drunk nor senile.

During my two-week visit to a small island town, Choroni caught my attention. The locals even helped me celebrate my birthday, which happened to fall on a Sunday. It was heartwarming to see the religious people of the town play music in the park on weeknights, but never on Sundays, which was surprising, and I was grateful.

Upon arriving at Choroni, a special little village in Venezuela, I was captivated by its beauty. As I got off the bus, I saw guys playing basketball on a court nearby and people coming and going from the parks. I began looking for a place to stay, and after some recommendations, research, and wandering around, I found a lovely bungalow-style home that locals rented out to tourists. The homes were colorful and cozy, and the locals were friendly and welcoming.

While exploring the village, I had the pleasure of meeting an old black musician who was in his 80s. He was a legend in the village, known for his Latin music. He spoke English and shared with me stories of his band days from the 1940s or 50s. He was a sweet person and left a lasting impression on me.

I was amazed how beautiful the beaches were. There was a cave system at the water line with perfectly calm water for swimming, and rock warmed by the sun to sit on. The water sparkling in the sun and the coolness while swimming in the caves were surreal. A tranquil moment, no bars, and no restaurants. I enjoyed it.

I loved my stay in a small cottage. The locals were warm and friendly, especially an old black musician in his 80s who spoke

English and shared his experiences of playing in bands from the 1940s or 50s.

One of the highlights of my stay was the music in the park during the week, particularly on Saturdays. The restaurants and coffee shops around the park also contributed to the lively atmosphere. However, the most unforgettable moment was when the locals played music for me on a Sunday, which was supposed to be a day of rest. I was so touched that people came out to celebrate my birthday, playing guitars, bongos, and drums. They even bought me drinks and wished me a happy birthday. It was an incredible experience that left me feeling like a rockstar.

After making some great acquaintances in Choroni, and feeling so much love from the strangers there, I returned to Maracaibo, the second largest city in Venezuela. I only stayed there for one night before heading back to Caracas, but I did take a walk around the city in the evening. There were many vendors, but I didn't know much about what was going on. I didn't do my due diligence and ended up wandering the streets aimlessly. Eventually, I returned to Caracas.

Venezuela has many interesting places to visit, including the mountains where cable cars take you up and over to the other. Additionally, the people of Venezuela are very attractive, and I wanted to learn more about their culture.

I was struck by the resilience of the Venezuelan people, both men and women, and found them to be very friendly. However, as I moved to the Caribbean side, my heart was filled with sadness due to the political situation in Venezuela and other parts of Central and South America. It's painful to see such beautiful countries with educated and sophisticated societies going through so much turmoil after Chavez. Despite this, I still believe Venezuela is a special place worth visiting, especially Choroni.

Thailand, Malaysia, Indonesia

Thailand: After finishing work in Hawaii, I frequently went on trips to explore new places. During the slow season, I traveled to South Korea. Later, I went to Bangkok, Thailand with a friend, and then went back alone for a second visit. I enjoyed it so much that I decided to go for a third time. Next, I went to Phuket Beach, Chiangmai, Pattaya, and KomSamui. Following that, I traveled to Bali, Indonesia.

Malaysia: I decided that I wanted to check out Kuala Lumpur in Malaysia, in the city I found the Muslim culture too restrictive for me. The women were covered completely from head to toe and walked three steps behind their husbands. Additionally, in that region the harvest was in, and the stubble in left in the fields was being burned to clear for the next planting. The countryside was filled with smoke, my eyes burned, and I couldn't breathe. I had to leave.

Indonesia: Then Indonesia beckoned me to Bali, with its dancing girls with clicking tongues and rhythmic head movements.

Bali has a unique artist town call UBUD where local artist's display all kinds of paintings and other crafts. There-is also a monkey farm where monkeys roam free and let themselves be fed by visitors.

Bali is a popular destination, and I was curious to explore what it had to offer. Depending on which area you visit, you can experience different customs and traditions. In one area, I observed girls clicking their tongues and making head movements.

In another area, there were monkey forests and artists who created beautiful butterfly art. I spent a month there, staying in a comfortable apartment with a balcony and a hammock. It was a great experience.

South America:
Brazil, Argentina, Uruguay, Columbia

Brazil: On my first trip to Rio de Janeiro, Brazil, I traveled with my friends. We finished working the Exotic Erotic Halloween Ball and were free to travel. Another friend of mine from New York, joined us, making it a group of four New Yorkers heading to Brazil.

We landed in Rio de Janeiro, a city with a diverse cultural potential. We stayed in Copacabana, a neighborhood popular with tourists who typically stay for two or three days, or sometimes a week as part of tour groups. It's all about tours and beaches, and the city caters to this clientele. Since we were new to Brazil, we didn't know much about other neighborhoods like Ipanema. If there was a show close to Copacabana, that's where we wanted to be. We Americans are familiar with the name Copacabana, and it's also where things were happening. But unfortunately, nothing really happened for us. On our first night, my friend Chris got into big trouble. I don't want to exaggerate, but it was funny in retrospect. We got dressed up for dinner, ready to explore Brazil. Dinner was nice and we were feeling good, so we returned to our hotel suite. There were three of us in the room and it was hot as hell that night, even though we had air conditioning. So, we went out looking for the party scene. We went to clubs and tried to find out what was going on, but we didn't really know where to go. At night, it's hard to figure out where the hotspots are. Instead, we encountered a lot of street people and prostitutes. Cars were passing by with their passengers seeking out nightlife and restaurants. It was hard to speak to anyone, and we felt lost in the city.

During our stay in Rios, Perry got into trouble. He picked up two women and brought them back to our hotel. Jeff was interested in one of the friends, but they seemed to be a package deal since one spoke English and the other didn't. While Jeff took one of the girls to a separate room, Perry was with the other in the main room. Suddenly, Perry screamed, and we all jumped up. It turned out that the girl he was with was actually a transvestite, which made Perry furious. The transvestite demanded to be paid. He's a New Yorker so he's going into "Oh, no, no, no, no, no, that just ain't going to happen." Then the girl says, "Yes, it is happening, you gonna pay me." Even though Perry didn't want to pay, we advised him to do so to avoid any further trouble. It was a lesson learned for us about being more cautious in Brazil and always checking and asking questions. The next day, we spent our time on the beach.

Figure 29 Christ the Redeemer

Calvin Campbell

I visited Coco Cabana Beach where topless was the norm. The beach was beautiful and great music and songs could be heard drifting from the bars on the broad walk. However, it was crowded with tourists, locals, and people seeking attention. We went on some tours around the city and mountains and spent about a week and a half in Rio, experiencing its unique vibe. On our last day, we stumbled upon Ipanema Beach, which was more our style. It was more high-end, less crowded, and had fewer people trying to sell us things. The atmosphere was more relaxed, and the beachgoers were more modestly dressed. They weren't wearing quite such revealing thongs, nor were the girls topless. We regretted not finding this perfect spot until our last day, it had a wonderful view of Rio behind us and the famous statue of Christ the

Redeemer on an island in the bay. We regretted finding this perfect spot on our last day, as it had a wonderful view of Christ the Redeemer statue and of a popular spot for paragliding, which I tried.

The hills behind Ipanema were a popular spot for paragliding, and I happened to meet a paragliding champion when I was at the Ceranda Retreat. He gave me a private lesson; I thought it might be fun to jump of a cliff and try flying. I was told that the secret was to catch the wind. Strapped into safety gear and the glider trailing behind, I missed the wind the first run, then I didn't make it the next two attempts either. People were running past me and jumping off the cliff edge, but not me. The wind always stopped when I got there. It might have been my Guardian Angels stopping the wind, it would have been thrilling if hadn't been so embarrassed and sweating way too much from fear. Nonetheless, we enjoyed the rest of our time in Brazil.

After leaving, Perry went back to his place in Hawaii, Pictures of Paradise. I returned to New York to finish school. Jeff returned to San Francisco, where he owned a night club. We are still friends to this day.

Having completed cosmetology school, I decided to pursue a career as an esthetician and enrolled at Christine Valmy, a well-regarded school where students wore white uniforms. It wasn't easy, but I enjoyed learning about anatomy, skin types, and skincare practices, including formulating different products. Once I obtained my esthetician's license, I decided it was time to celebrate, so I returned to Rio de Janeiro, but this time on my own. I decided to skip Copacabana and head straight to Ipanema, where I felt more at home and could avoid the crowds and constant selling.

I left Rio and went on a trip of discovery.

The Bahia the State, and Salvador the main city, were both incredible. I got to see an amazing rich diverse culture and a large population of people of African descent from the large plantation era. The city of Salvador has impressive architecture, and a happy, easy going, lifestyle.

However, I couldn't help but notice the lack of black people in upscale malls working in visible positions. Although there were some working in housekeeping and kitchen positions, I rarely saw them behind the counter or serving customers. When I went to upscale restaurants in Rio de Janeiro and Ipanema, I made a conscious effort to study the lack of diversity. Despite being an American, I still experienced some racism in nightclubs, although being an English-speaking American gave me more privileges than Afro-Brazilians. The currency of money mattered more than race, but the undertone of racism was still present.

Argentina: During my time in Argentina, I didn't come across many Black people. I heard that they were often placed on the front lines during the war. However, I did observe Black people practicing yoga, and someone pointed out their presence and asked why I was noticing them. Generally speaking, in many South American countries, black people hold positions in middle management or work in truck driving, security, or restaurants.
As an African American, I am familiar with the hierarchy and color lines, and I observed these in Central and South America. I also noted that many Afro-Latinos are no longer identifying as Latino due to the problematic history between Latinos and black people. Instead, they are identifying as Afro-Colombian, Afro-Panamanian, Afro-Brazilian, or another identifier that highlights their African descent. This is especially true in countries like Brazil, where slavery had a significant impact.

In Colombia, there are still pockets of darker-skinned individuals in places like Cali, but few hold high positions in areas like Bogota. I tried to observe the demographics in various places, such as clubs, hotels, supermarkets, public transportation, and upscale neighborhoods. I had an incident in Medellin where the police stopped me several times in two weeks while I was staying in an upscale Airbnb in a nice neighborhood. However, once they realized I was a foreigner living in the area, they treated me differently. While I love Medellin, it's essential to observe things as they are rather than how we want them to be. It's important to acknowledge our identities as Afro-Americans, Afro-Brazilians, Afro-Colombians, etc., but also recognize the racial dynamics in Central and South America.

After traveling to Brazil several times, I developed an interest in visiting Argentina - a country often referred to as the Europe of South America. The concept of experiencing Europe in Argentina intrigued me, particularly since tango dancing is one of their most popular exports, and they're reputed to have handsome men due to the mix of Spanish and Italian heritage.

During the 1930s and 40s, many Italians migrated to Argentina, making it the most popular place to be in South America. It wasn't a jungle or primitive place; instead, it was very upscale, like Europe. I wanted to witness this firsthand, so I planned my visit in January when the country experiences summer. January is also when all the events and festivities are in full swing, making it the perfect time to visit.

One of the places I was keen on exploring was the Piazza del Mayo Street, a popular attraction in Buenos Aires, the capital of Argentina. I also wished to visit a synagogue that had been bombed and was in the newspapers. The bombing incident was a horrific experience, especially since it occurred before it became common to bomb religious places. Buenos Aires, being the largest and most popular city, was also the most fashionable city in Argentina.

While there, I attended a class that taught various Latin dances like samba, tango, moringa, and cha-cha. I tried them all, but the tango was the most popular, and I did well. However, since Buenos Aires is a vast city, I didn't stay there for too long. Instead, I heard about a resort area called Punta Del Este, located in Uruguay. I was fascinated by the yachts, boats, and jet skis that people owned in this area, and it was supposed to be upscale and luxurious. It's where most South Americans with money vacation, and Argentinians take their vacations there while Brazilians prefer to stay in their areas.

However, one thing that disappointed me about Argentina was the lack of people of color. I barely saw any black folks or people of color. While driving in the countryside, I did spot people with black ancestry due to their features, but it wasn't a common sight. It was a mixture of Spanish and Italian heritage. I eventually left Argentina and visited Uruguay, a place with a liberal mindset and representation of black people, although still not many people of color.

Overall, my trip to both countries lasted less than a month, and I stayed mostly on the coasts. Although I enjoyed the experience, I didn't see anything that made me want to stay longer or go back. But every time you go, you see something different, you meet new people who show you something different, another energy, another spirit. What I saw in my three weeks of traveling alone, I didn't see anything that said, "Stay, stay, stay", even the partying.

Spain

My first trip to Spain I met a girl who worked at a bar, and we hit it off, partying and having a good time. She borrowed some money from me and asked me to collect it the next morning when she got paid. However, the next day, I was scared when I saw her without her ponytail and eyebrows, wearing a raggedy robe and looking tired. Though she wanted me to come inside, I couldn't. I politely declined.

Overall, I enjoyed my trip and came back to the States feeling frisky.

I went back to Spain and accepted an invitation from a friend to stay in Palma de Majorca for a while. Although I found Madrid to be just another bustling city where I felt lost and uninterested, I eventually discovered that Ibiza was the ultimate party destination. I took a ferry that ran between Las Palmas and Ibiza, and the experience made the island feel like a separate entity. Ibiza has ferry's that take you to other islands and to Spain, a castle that attracts many European vacationers, and a lively disco scene that primarily draws in Germans and Swedes.

During my travels, I learned to distinguish between the Spanish from Barcelona and those from other parts of Spain. As I spent time walking around and speaking Spanish, I noticed differences in their accents. I particularly enjoyed my time in Catalonia and stayed there for several weeks before moving on to Greece, stopping in Ibiza.

Ibiza: Let me share with you one of my favorite destinations in Europe that holds a special place in my heart - Ibiza. This stunning island off the coast of Spain is truly unparalleled. If you're a fan of partying, soaking up the sun, exploring scenic mountain roads on a motorcycle, and meeting people from around the world, then Ibiza is the perfect place for you. During the end-of-summer season, young people from all corners of Europe, including Sweden, Germany, Italy, and other unknown places, flock to Ibiza.

I reached this beautiful island by taking a ferry that operates multiple times a day from Palma de Majorca. Upon arrival, my eyes were drawn to a massive castle resembling a Roman fortress that closes at night. However, upon entering, it transformed into a charming little village with cobblestone streets, shops, and boutiques. I spent a delightful two weeks on this island where every night was a party, while the days were spent lounging on the beach. As the afternoon approached, people would start drinking and searching for food while the streets echoed with music, and vendors offered exciting excursions to explore.

If you venture into Ibiza's Old Town, you will find neighborhoods of shops where you can indulge in almost any city activity. Like all ancient Mediterranean cities, the port is on the sea plane, and the original old town is built on a nearby hill for protection. The Old Town is the hub of the party scene. The boat docks, the hotels, the restaurants in fact everything is within walking distance in Ibiza making it an easy and accessible place explore.

People from all over Europe come to party on the island. However, you don't see many people from Central and South America, except for Brazil. There are some Africans and people with darker skin, but they are a minority compared to the partying population. I went to Ibiza for its legendary party scene a few times in the late 90s, and it was always a wild experience. It's possible that the scene has become more diverse since then. The party atmosphere was so addictive that I found myself returning every summer. After Ibiza, I traveled to Majorca, and from there, I went to Madrid, which is a bustling city with a main boulevard and all that. When I was in Ibiza, I learned a lot about the different people from Spain and all over Europe who come to the island to party.

I was struck by how Catalonians had a distinct accent that set them apart from people in Madrid or other parts of Spain. The difference in tone was remarkable, and even though there may be words in the United States that have regional variations, the contrast in Spain felt like a different race of people within the same country, like the north and south accents in the US.

It was a beautiful experience to be able to discern where people came from, even if you didn't know their specific location, as you could hear the different cultures reflected in their speech. Spain and Italy shared similarities in terms of culture, sophistication, elegance, and glamour, to party and have fun everyone likes.

Portugal: Lisbon, Portugal marks the beginning of a dark history of human enslavement. Portugal was a notorious colonizer that dominated Brazil, Mozambique, and many other countries. Intrigued by this past, I visited Lisbon to see if there were any monuments or symbols that acknowledge their involvement in the slave trade. The city surprised me with its stunning waterfront, adorned with a massive plaza and 17th century buildings. I was also impressed by the unique streetcar that roamed the town, as well as the charming blue and white tile artworks that adorned buildings.

Staying in the old part of Lisbon, I explored its cobblestoned streets and discovered many hidden restaurants and gay bars where I met friendly locals. As a tourist, I found plenty of art that showcased the city's creativity, but I couldn't find any areas where black people lived. Despite encountering black people in bars, I was unable to locate a black-owned neighborhood where I could taste their food and listen to their music. This absence bothered me, and I wished to witness the quality of life of black people in Portugal and compare it to that of other parts of the world, particularly other regions of the Diaspora.

It's worth noting that Portugal's history of slavery is one of many. The Spanish, French, Germans, and Americans all played their part in the colonization and enslavement of black people. Brazil, for example, had no white women until the queen of Portugal arrived, and prior to that, only white men and enslaved black women existed in the country. Overall, I found Lisbon to be historically intriguing, but I'm uncertain if I'll ever return.

Greece

Greece: Mykonos, Greece was an amazing destination with its striking white buildings. One could take small boats to the neighboring islands in the morning, which were renowned for their nude beaches. There were even some cafes and rocky areas where people would sit nude and have lunch. It was a place where everyone was nude, except for a few who preferred to wear clothes. The nude culture was the main attraction for people to come here, and I have visited a few such places before, including one in Miami. However, the Mykonos experience was unique, where people respected each other's privacy and didn't judge or stare.

At night, I would party and make new acquaintances, such as a lady who had a husband traveling to London during the week, leaving her alone. We would spend time together during the week, and her husband had invited me to London, which was lovely to hear. Spain, Greece, and London were all inexpensive destinations, which suited me well as I always travel on a budget. As a nomadic traveler, I look for clean accommodations and good local food that is inexpensive. I believe ambiance and the people around me are more important than the quality of food. If the atmosphere is great, I don't mind if the food is just okay.

England, France

During my first trip to London, England, I stayed with my friend's parents in Finsbury Park, a working-class area inhabited by both English and Polish people. I found his mother to be the most intriguing individual since she had migrated to London from Poland after the war. She informed me that regardless of how long anyone lived in London or England, they would never be considered British. I listened attentively to her stories about the war and her experiences, and it was a touching experience.

While staying with them, I connected well with my friend's sister, who developed a fondness for me. She would insist that I stay and chat with her instead of leaving to explore. I would occasionally explore London, travelling by train to visit places such as Piccadilly Circus, Hyde Park, Chelsea, and other notable destinations.

I would walk through the West End, past palaces, and the barracks of the Queen's Guards. I watched them ride horses through the streets, in the red uniforms and silver and gold helmets with horsehair plumes. I would take the train to Piccadilly Circus and Hyde Park before heading over to Chelsea. I would often head to the local High Street to unwind and visit bars in the afternoon, which became a bit rowdier as the day wore on. I particularly enjoyed the London Underground, which they affectionately call the "Tube". I was so taken with London that I ended up staying for six months, mostly due to meeting someone who lived in Mayfair, and we often talked about Italy.

Eventually, I left London and travelled to Germany, specifically to Munich.

France: I was in Paris for a fragrance company meeting, after work we would go out on the town. The Louvre Museum had so many beautiful things that I grew up hearing about, like the Mona Lisa which I was finally seeing. The food everywhere was fabulous, and the pastries were delish. The Champs Elise had many boutiques, and most of them were the work showrooms for known designers, I was elated at being in close contact with so many talented people. I loved France and imagined how incredible it must have been before World War II.

South America: Columbia - Panama

Every time I travel to Central or South America, and other places of the diaspora, I always have in the back of my mind to check how black people were treated. I wanted to see if the society accepted them. I wanted to really check out the Afro Latino. At some point, however, I stopped calling them Afro Latino and started calling them Afro Columbian. I feel that being black coming out slavery in the Americas, has affected us all. This true whether you're in America, in Central America, or South

America, or in parts of Africa, we have all been affected by slavery, its remnants, and the trauma of having slave ancestry. When I was in Colombia, I may have resided in an upscale area, but I definitely spent a lot of my time trying to be local and seek out the local atmosphere.

Black people are there. I find in Colombia, black and brown hang out together and everything is cool, you are like family, you are like brothers. But once you get into being white, that European looking white, that Spanish looking white, then I find a bigger gap between African, Latino, African Dominican or African Colombian. I find that that line becomes greater when added to the class system, the lighter you are the sometimes the better off you are. You can blend in. The darker you are doesn't mean in those countries you feel ostracized, you sort of know your place.

I saw a lot of the blacks in Colombia. In Cartagena they had good jobs, but more of the mediocre jobs, the labor jobs, or they were selling things. Very few were in high end, and they were generally the younger generations. I could go into a coffee shop and see a black girl behind the counter, only as stock people. In the Old City it was common to see blacks and whites patronizing the same clubs. On those social levels there was a lot of mixing. But in business, there's a hierarchy and color barrier. Certain businesses, like banking, you see fewer blacks, and more "high yellow" and whites.

Figure 31 Cartagena Columbia

Figure 30 Cartagena Columbia

Calvin Campbell

Cartagena

Figure 32 Scenes from my windows

Panama: If you are of African descent, it may be challenging to gain entry to nightclubs and upscale restaurants without a tourist or foreigner accompanying you. I could sense that my friend would not have been permitted inside without me. I observed a similar situation in Panama, where I resided as a permanent resident for several years. Although I did not encounter as much racism there, I did notice some remnants of it while visiting casinos in Panama City. Even though it wasn't as overt as in other Latin American countries, I could still feel its presence.

During my time in Panama, I stayed for nearly seven years, which was longer than any other place I've lived. I also ran a guest house for five years, called "Free Spirit Inn," on the island of Bastimentos Island, which was only accessible by launcher boats that functioned like taxis, a ten-minute ride. Many locals worked in Bocas del Toro but resided in places like Red Frog, Carneiro, or any of the islands in the chain. The taxi boat business's rush hour was typically from five to seven, but boats were available day and night.

If you need a launcher (small boat) from a club in Bocas, you can easily call one on the phone, even on a Sunday or when working late at night. You can find one or two launchers waiting outside the club for partygoers who need a ride back to places like Carneiro, Bastimentos, or Red Frog Beach. Typically, I would leave around eight or nine o'clock from Bastimentos and take a water taxi. However, if you wait until later in the evening, there are fewer available. On Friday and Saturday nights, the boats are in high demand and plentiful, so you don't have to wait long at the dock.

BASTIMENTOS ISLAND
BOCAS DEL TORO, PANAMA

GUESTHOUSE & NATURE MEDITATION TOURS
OUR ECO FRIENDLY INN OFFERS
COMFORTABLE SUITES WITH DREAMY BEDS,
PRIVATE BATHROOMS WITH HOT SHOWERS
AND STONE MASSAGE FLOORS.
THERE IS A MEDITATION HUT ON THE
PROPERTY & HAMMOCKS & OUT-DOOR GRILL
EACH SUITE HAS A BALCONY VIEW OF
NEARBY ISLANDS IN THE BAY.

FREE SPIRIT
INN

This is the history and the unique benefits of Bastimentos Island compared to the other islands. Bastimentos is one of the oldest and largest islands in the area, as many people settled there after the abolition of slavery to work on building roads or on the Panama Canal. Others worked on the many banana, pineapple, and mango plantations, which shipped their products out of the nearby port of Amaranth.

Many of the people who work at the port live in nearby areas like Amaranth, Bocos, Bastimentos, or Carnerio.

Historically, most Panamanian people originated from the Caribbean, as there was a demand for labor in Panama, and the Panamanians allowed them to come and work. Over the course of a century, many Jamaicans decided to stay. During the turn of the century, people of color began to arrive, including Chinese immigrants. This created a cultural blend of Chinese, Black, and Latino populations.

While residing in Bastimentos, I constructed both my home and guest house from the ground up. I collaborated with an architect and employed indigenous individuals to assist with the building process. We opted for thatched roofs and large posts to support the upper and lower levels. When it rains in Panama, people tend to spend their time playing backgammon, enjoying drinks, or listening to music on the upper floor, while sleeping on the lower level.

The local culture in Bastimentos Island may have been influenced by the island's natural environment, particularly the frequent rains that can keep people indoors for days. When building my home and guest house, I considered the need for good lighting, mirrors, and hot showers to make the indoor experience more comfortable. I also had a garden where I attempted to grow pineapples but instead grew peppers and sunflowers.

The place where I resided was a jungle, with dirt paths and only a few concrete structures near the bottom of the hill. My guest house was not just a building in the jungle but rather part of the jungle path itself, as I wanted to honor the natural surroundings.

If you need medical care or want to do any shopping, Bocas is the place to go. The airport is within sight, and you can find government offices, churches, and large hotels in the area. Bocas town is like a mini-city or town, while Carson Invokes town is also nearby. You can take a ferry boat from Volkers to Amaranta on the mainland and catch a bus to Panama City or other places.

Since Bocas is an island, you need to take a car ferry to Amaranta to get buses or taxis to other destinations.

Figure 33 Waterside homes

To cook outside, a friend and I built a stone grill and a nearby teepee-style seating area that could accommodate up to 12 people. The guest house had six rooms, which I rented out to European and American tourists, as many Panamanian tourists found it too expensive and preferred to stay in more central locations.

Figure 34 A main street parade - Panamanian cowboys

Figure 35 A main street parade - Panamanian cowboys

Although I enjoyed living in my home and guest house, I regret not building a tree house with a panoramic view. I relied on a nearby well for water, as the island experiences both dry and wet seasons. I also had various amenities for guests, such as hammocks, rocking chairs, and a smoke hut for smokers. My dog Lucy was a loyal companion and protector of my guests, distinguishing between locals and tourists by her behavior towards them.

I miss Lucy and my guest house, but I had to sell it. Like many things in life, I couldn't expect anyone else to care for it with the same passion as I did. I had to undergo a minor surgery in the US, so I asked my European friend to manage it while I recovered. During that time, the reviews were great, and everyone loved my place. People took pictures, and the feedback was excellent. However, my friend didn't have the same passion as I did, and some customers began to complain about cleanliness. Instead of allowing complaints to tarnish my reputation, I decided to sell the property. I had two choices: either return and run it myself or entrust it to someone who might not share my love and dedication for it. I chose to sell because I believe that no one could care for it as I did.

Panama boasts a variety of environments. During my trip, I first stayed in Panama City, which is perfect for tourists wanting to visit the Panama Canal or enjoy entertainment options like

Figure 36 Waterfall in the Highlands jungle of Boquete Panama

casinos, clubs, and restaurants. They also have a mall near the airport for those who want to shop. Panama City has a business area and a banking area where all the banks are located. I enjoyed my time in the upscale area of Panama City, but I didn't want to stay too long as it lacked a certain exotic flavor that I was seeking. The people were nice, but not as interesting or edgy.

After I sold my guest house on Bastimentos Island. I moved to David, the county city of Chroni in the north of Panama. David is the largest city in this area and is one of the top cities in Panama. However, I found David to be too hot for my liking even though I don't mind the heat. I rented a nice house there for a year, but I didn't find it had much to offer me during my time there. They do have events like flower festivals and cowboys come into town for a parade, but that's about it.

There are many exciting events happening in Panama City such as the casino, baseball games, and various festivals, but the extreme heat can make it uncomfortable and lacking in distinctive character. As a result, I decided to venture to Boquete, a mountainous area popular among foreigners, who can afford to live in exotic and stunning locations alongside the locals. The locals from places like Panama City and Boquete, however, cannot afford to enjoy the same luxuries for extended periods of time.

Boquete offers a plethora of activities such as rafting, rock climbing, mud healing, massages, and reflexology. You can also purchase fresh fruits and meats, including chickens, from the local truck vendors, as well as handmade items such as machetes, fabric, wool, and indigenous art. Boquete is well known for its wildflowers and orchards. Orchards are everywhere. It truly has everything you need.

Figure 37 Rock climbing in Boquete

Boquete has a unique and distinct flavor that is completely different from other places in Panama. Its landscape is breathtaking, with coffee plantations and wildflowers adding to the visual appeal of the place. The elevation of Boquete allows one to feel close to the stars at night, which are brighter due to the low light pollution. The weather is perfect, with eternal spring making it never too hot or too cold. While a sweater or jacket may be needed at night, during the day. It's usually warm unless it's the rainy season, which is a warm rain and pleasant. There are many farmers in Boquete who have coffee fields and vineyards for wine.

What makes Boquete even more special are the indigenous people going about their daily lives, shopping or working, along with their children. There are many restaurants in Boquete that are uniquely set in stone, and quaint cafes with beautiful flower gardens are common. Boquete is there. It's an upper-middle-class area, where backpackers and locals come weekends as a way of getting out of David. On Saturday night, they have the bars and restaurants for tourists. It's a destination place to eat, go to clubs or go to the bars because it's cooler.

Boquete has everything one could need, including banking services. Many (expats) Americans, Brits and French are living year-round in Boquete. The city is more elegant than other places like David. Tourists and locals come for day trips or weekend as a special destination. The Tuesday Market is always busy, packed with everything from arts and crafts to exotic local food. The good thing is everyone goes there so you are sure to meet friends shopping.

During my stay in Boquete, I enjoyed my time and found it to be a great place for creativity. Additionally, it's conveniently located near the airport in David, making it easy to fly to places like Panama City. While the bus ride to Panama City is long and takes an overnight trip, a flight takes less than an hour.

There is also a place called Red Frog which is an upscale area on an island with a beach where many tourists have big homes or rent for the season. Every island has its own upscale area, some are only for working while others allow you to live with the locals, like where I did. There are also small jungle places where you can live by yourself. Anyway, that's my story for Panama. I am a permanent resident of Panama so I can go back and forth, and it also allows me to travel to other places in Central America such as Colombia. In case you didn't know, Panama is in Central America where the famous Panama Canal can be found.

During my 2023 visit to Panama, I realized many young adults there dream of going to America, the land of opportunity, but they do not put in the effort to learn English. While discussing my book on travel, which they found useful, I discovered that they have very little knowledge of geography. They are unaware of country names, pronunciations, capital cities, and even what the people of certain countries are called. For instance, they didn't know that people from Finland are called "Fins," from Denmark are called "Danes," and from England are called "Brits." They are also unfamiliar with various currencies and how to budget while traveling. Learning even a few words of the language of the country you plan to visit would be found very useful.

Bocas del Toro is a tourist destination, attracting visitors for surfing, diving, snorkeling, and other water sports. There are private boats available, and you can explore caves and other attractions in the area.

Africa: Northern

Morocco: Part of what was once called the French Sahara the city of Casablanca has always intrigued me. Ever since seeing Aladdin as a child, and then later Lawrence of Arabia and Casablanca (with Bogart and Bacall) memorable movies of a lifetime, I have dreamed of Morocco. The old section of Casablanca, Derb Ghallef is worth a visit. Built long before the French got there and transformed Casablanca into a French Colonial city.

Marrakech: As I was planning to leave Casablanca, I met a university student who spoke English and a couple of other languages, he agreed to help me out to come with to get me comfortable in this beautiful city because my French is very limited.

Marrakesh bright pink walled medieval city, to this day is the trading center for the Berbers in the desert, was unreal. The train ride from Casablanca to Marrakech was hot but he and I stood between the train cars to get some cool air and to see the countryside, it was amazing. What an amazing city. With its narrow streets and mosaic style architecture is spectacularly beautiful. It is my favorite architectural art form. I loved the fountains and Bahia palaces. I was invited to visit homes with beautiful courtyard gardens. The best experience was at night at Jemaah El Fnaa, the night market , with food stalls , and entertainment with a lot of different performers doing acts right on Berber. People were selling traditional textiles and jewelry, the Moorish minaret of 12th century, so much history with a great monument going back to the 12th century. I didn't study that in high school in the Bronx.

Thus far, I have made eight trips to Africa traveling to Morocco, Egypt twice, South Africa, Mozambican, Ghana, Ivory Coast, and Ethiopia. My second and adventurous trip to Africa was to Egypt. I stopped in Cairo, which was a busy and chaotic city with traffic jams. However, I visited Giza, where the pyramids are located, and that was a thrilling experience. It was my first time riding a camel, and I went into the pyramids and explored the tombs. Going down the little stairs into the tombs was eerie yet amazing, as I could feel the dry air and was surrounded by the body of a pyramid that was thousands of years old. I also saw a perfumery where they made natural oils and even made my own fragrance. Before leaving Giza, I rode a donkey and a camel and witnessed the beautiful sunrise and stars in the desert. Giza is a must-see place in Egypt, and I highly recommend it. I think my second trip to Egypt, I stayed there for a year. During that trip, I visited the museums in Cairo, which showcase a lot of Egyptian history, including mummies and the different dynasties of pharaohs. While Cairo is a place to visit for a few days, I found it too hectic, and I moved on to Luxor.

Luxor is a stunning place with, having the Valley of the Kings as a bonus, a plethora of old museums and an abundance of historical landmarks. There is another side of Luxor which is more residential and to reach it, one can take a boat such as a ferry boat or a gondola to navigate across. Alternatively, one can take a ferry bus used by daily commuters who work on one side and live on the other. During my stay, I also visited Shama Shek, a popular tourist destination and location for many international government meetings. Moving on, I traveled to Aswan, which is where you can find the Nubian people who live on the borders of Sudan. Although I wanted to go to Sudan, I did not have the necessary visa and so I stayed in Aswan, which is located on the Nile.

I learned about the history of race and culture in Egypt during my travels. The Nubian people, who are black, have experienced discrimination from the government, which has tried to force them off their land near the Nile. As I traveled from Luxor down to Aswan, I noticed that the people became progressively darker in skin tone. This is likely due to the influence of Romans who mixed with the locals during their long reign over Egypt over the course of several centuries. Despite this diversity, I found that the Egyptian culture was still very prevalent throughout the country.

One of my favorite places to stay was Dahab, which is situated on the Nile and provided a relaxing and authentic Egyptian experience. The restaurants in Dahab are unique, with seating on the floor and shisha pipes for smoking. There are also opportunities for adventure, such as camel rides and paragliding. The bungalows in Dahab are made of stone and add to the overall experience of staying there.

Figure 38 A friend's newly built home in Luxor, Egypt

Each place in Egypt has its own unique flavor, geared towards tourism. Dahab is a more touristy place, with more innovative and creative housing options for tourists. However, Egypt is amazing, and I had the opportunity to live there for a year. I traveled from Northern Cyprus, where I had a condo, to escape the cold and rainy winter weather. I stayed in Cairo for a week, then moved to Luxor for a month, and went on excursions to places like Sharm El Sheikh, Aswan, and Dahab. Egypt's history and culture are fascinating, but the weather can be extremely hot during the day. People often come out early in the morning to do their shopping before retreating indoors during the hottest part of the day. Everything reopens in the evening when the heat has subsided. Despite the weather, Egypt is a must-visit destination.

Egypt is a mystical place where one can feel a strong spiritual energy. The stars are brighter there than anywhere else I've seen, and the desert is so peaceful. I even started dressing like the locals, wearing a "gallabiyah" and sometimes a turban on my head. The people were also very friendly, with many young Egyptians calling me "cousin" and making me feel like family. While some may have reservations about Egypt and Africa, I never had any problems and found the Egyptian men to be good-looking and natural. They tend to have a more traditional lifestyle, with wives staying at home to take care of the children and household duties. However, when they meet Western women, they are more open and flirtatious, as they enjoy the novelty of the interaction. Although drinking alcohol is generally forbidden in Egyptian culture, the hotels that cater to tourists have bars and clubs where locals can also drink if accompanied by a foreigner. It's accepted in these settings, and no one judges or looks down upon them.

During my time in Egypt, I tried to experience as much as possible. I visited both the mosque and the Coptic church, wanting to immerse myself in the culture and represent the diversity of my family. I felt honored when the locals referred to me as "cousin," as it indicated a sense of kinship and acceptance. One of the highlights of my trip was taking a Palooka boat on the Nile, where I had a guide who not only steered the sailboat but also made coffee. It was a unique and special experience that I will always cherish. As a foreigner, I can attest to the country's magical atmosphere and can understand why people feel compelled to return.

If given the opportunity, I highly recommend visiting Egypt. Egyptian people are warm, friendly, and enjoy interacting with tourists and foreigners. They appreciate the cultural exchange that comes with hosting visitors and are eager to share their country with others.

Exploring the Valley of the Kings is a treat for locals as well, as some may not have had the chance to visit due to the cost of admission to many museums and galleries. Luxor at night is also a unique experience, with people walking along the promenade, enjoying ice cream and the waterfront restaurants. The parks are lively and safe, and there are many events to take part in after the sun goes down.

Egypt has a rich history and culture, with fascinating details about pharaohs, queens, and kings that are worth learning about. It was once a united land that included the modern-day regions in Africa and North Africa. During my time there, I was able to gain a deeper understanding of the history and culture of Egypt, and even discovered that some pharaohs looked like me due to the influence of Nubia. Queen of Sheba and King Solomon also have connections to Egypt, making it an even more interesting place to explore.

I cannot recommend Egypt enough, and I am certain that my love for the country will continue to grow. The Egyptians have embraced me as family, and I am grateful for the experiences I have had in this historically rich and visually stunning place. It truly is a once-in-a-lifetime destination that should be on everyone's travel list.

Out of all my travels to Africa, the experience that impacted me the most and helped me grow as a person was my trip to Ghana, particularly because of its connection to the slave trade. The Cape Coast in Ghana was one of the major sites of the slave trade, where the El Mina Castle housed many of the slaves who were transported to America, Jamaica, the Caribbean, and Brazil through the Portuguese, Dutch, English, French, Spanish, and German traders.

As an African American, it was especially meaningful for me to visit The Cape Coast and see the dungeons where my ancestors were held captive for months, waiting to be shipped to the Americas. The slaves were chained together in the dark, cramped dungeon, with almost 1000 of them packed into one space. The only light came from a small window high up on the dungeon ceiling, which was not meant for ventilation but just to let in a little light.

Learning about the hardship, pain, and suffering that my ancestors faced was a difficult experience during my visit to The Cape Coast in Ghana. Prior to their capture, my ancestors were not slaves, but rather workers, kings, and queens. Those who were captured were usually prisoners of war from losing tribes. If the Europeans were interested in buying a slave or servant, they would be taken to the market. The mentality of the African tribes who won the war was to get rid of their enemies, which allowed the Arabs to trade and the Europeans to buy slaves as product. Taking advantage of the situation.

My trip to Ghana was especially important to me, as it was for notable figures such as President Obama and Beyonce, due to its historical significance as a major slave trade site. Hearing about the experiences of my ancestors and their struggles was a powerful and eye-opening experience.

Ghana is a destination that every African American, and in fact, every American should visit to witness the suffering endured by those who were captured and transferred onto ships through "the door of no return." This door was so narrow that only one person could pass through at a time, and it was designed to prevent mutiny. These individuals did not want to be enslaved or leave their continent and some chose to jump overboard. They were dealing with a new and unfamiliar group of people, white people.

161

During my trip to Ghana, the experience really hit me hard. There is a church, believed to have been built by the Portuguese, right beside the dungeons. I was told that people used to come out of the church and throw food down into the dungeon, which was barbaric. It is shocking that these individuals claimed to be Christians with love in their hearts. The church is still located on the same property as the dungeons, and the memory of it left me feeling sickened.

Figure 39 Standing outside the Holy Trinity Church in Addis Abba Ethiopia

Figure 40 King and Queen of Ethiopia

Another place that deeply impacted me and reminded me of the resilience and strength of African history and culture is Ethiopia. Unlike many other African countries, Ethiopia has not been colonized or enslaved by Europeans. It's a country in East Africa that I used to hear about as a child, with stories of powerful queens, like Sheba, and King Solomon. Ethiopian is an old language and Ethiopia is also the birthplace of coffee and the place where the Menglik, son of the Queen of Sheba & King Soloman, brought the Ark of the Covenant to Ethiopia in 586 BC.

What I love about Ethiopia is that it allows us to go back to a time before European influence, to a time when African culture was thriving and authentic. Ethiopia's language and religion go back thousands of years, with Christianity being established there long before it was in Europe. The Ethiopian cross, known as the Coptic Cross, has a unique design and holds a special place in my heart, as I have one of my own.

Figure 41 Standing before the longest limo I have ever seen.

Calvin Campbell

Figure 42 An amazing site in Ethiopia. In the 1950s Selassie gave 404 retired solders, who had fought in the war against the Italian colonization, plots of land to farm. They came with their families and settled in what was then near a small town called Adare. It grew into what is now the regional capital renamed Hawassa.

165

Figure 43 Coffee station in a hotel lobby of building

Even though some may argue that being colonized would have improved Ethiopia's position, I see it as a country that embodies our past without the influence of European colonization.

Ethiopia is a growing city with charming and beautiful people, although there are conflicts that have been present since I was thirteen years old. I learned about Emperor Haile Selassie of Ethiopia, and for the first time, discovered that black people have a past that goes back thousands of years, a civilization, and a rich history that predates slavery and the Underground Railroad.

Ethiopia is notable for, at one point, having had a cabinet in which 50% of the members were Ethiopian women, and the Vice President was also a woman.

Ethiopia's judicial system is remarkable, with the head of the judiciary being a woman, is an outstanding accomplishment for the country. In fact, I don't know of any European countries that have achieved this. Ethiopia is currently working to help 30,000 homeless children and those who have been abused. I strongly support their efforts. If any of my friends share my sentiments, I urge you to support Ethiopia too. Although Ethiopia has faced many challenges over the centuries, it is still worth our support. Ethiopia is dear to me, and I believe it is part of our future and our path to celebrate.

Ghana: The Gold Coast, Ghana is the world's second-largest exporter of cocoa. In 2017, the West African country produced an estimated 909,493 metric tons of cocoa, marking the largest harvest in six years. However, it is surprising to note that Africans consume only 4% of chocolate products from the continent. Ghana Cocoa Processing Company Limited is responsible for the production of the country's popular Golden Tree chocolate, which is readily available on every shelf and sold in the streets of the country. The company processes approximately 65,000 metric tons of premium Ghana cocoa beans annually in its factories.

In a bid to increase the local consumption of cocoa products from the world's second-largest producer of the crop, Ghana's President, Nana Addo Dankwa Akufo-Addo, has promised to launch a program that will provide every Ghanaian student with a bar of chocolate or cocoa beverage daily while in school. The government agencies are tasked with ensuring that cocoa beverages and chocolates are consistently provided to school children from primary to secondary levels. This decision is part of the government's plan to promote the consumption of cocoa products locally.

Ghana is one of the souls of West Africa and is often overlooked by hurried travelers who seek to do and see everything. However, spending a week in Ghana can provide a truly unique and immersive experience that allows visitors to fully appreciate and understand the culture. We take a different approach to traditional group tours that focus on ticking off tourist attractions, cramming into crowded buses, and following patronizing guides. Instead, we prefer to travel like locals, discovering new people, sampling local eateries, and staying in small hotels. Our goal is to capture moments that leave us feeling rejuvenated, grateful, and inspired, rather than simply checking items off a list.

Our trips prioritize forging meaningful connections and friendships. Although some of our participants may not usually enjoy group travel, we attract like-minded, kind, and adventurous individuals who want to make the most of their time on Earth.

What can you expect from a trip to Ghana with us? First, you will discover the city in a way that goes beyond typical tourist experiences. You will have the opportunity to dine with locals and immerse yourself in authentic Ghanaian culture. Our professional photographer will accompany you, capturing every moment so that you can relax and enjoy your trip without worrying about taking pictures. We also provide local guides, customized arrival instructions (in case you want to explore independently before the trip), and a Free Spirit Planet team member to ensure that everything runs smoothly. You spend a significant amount of time helping others, working hard, and managing your daily responsibilities. It's time to allow someone else to take care of you.

While I am creating a plan to offer guided tours, I understand that not everyone will be interested in the Ghana trip or any other destination. This is because our travel experiences are about spending time with remarkable people from around the globe and exploring new destinations with someone who understands the culture and terrain. Our tours provide unparalleled experiences that cannot be found in guidebooks. You can simply arrive, and we will have everything arranged for you.

With a decade of traveling experience under my belt, I know what it takes to have a great time no matter where you are, and now you can too. They say that it's not what you know, it's who you know, and we have cultivated incredible relationships with locals over the years who you will have the pleasure of meeting because we consider them friends. This means that you will also receive top-notch food and services because you are with us.

Imagine exploring the world with a well-traveled friend who knows about the best food and views each destination has to offer. Our team is extremely positive, supportive, grounded, and drama-free. We truly understand your desires and aspirations. We know what you want to see, do, and experience because we were once vacationers too. The only difference is that we now have the means to navigate like locals, giving you the best-of-both-worlds experience with our unique perspective.

During my visit to Accra - Ghana, the capital city, I witnessed a remarkable display of Ghana's culture of unity. On a designated Friday of every month, people from all walks of life - street vendors, office workers, businesspeople - proudly wear African clothing. This was a beautiful and awe-inspiring sight. Interestingly, Ghana is one of the few countries where African Americans can acquire citizenship after four years of residency. In the past, with just $500, one could instantly obtain citizenship and start a business, own property, or receive healthcare without a Ghanaian partner. It appears that Ghana is moving forward, leaving its past behind.

Addis, Ethiopia holds a special place in my heart as it is the home of the African Union headquarters and a place where the soul of my African history resides. Despite facing issues like wars, poverty, and cultural conflicts, I witnessed a great deal of love, warmth, and care for one another among the Ethiopian people. Ethiopia has a long history dating back thousands of years, which has not been colonized by outsiders. The country's language was both written and spoken, and it is believed that Ethiopia was where the Romans brought Christian religion and the covenant.

The legend is that Priests escaped with the Ark of the Covenant when Jerusalem was under siege by the Babylonians and delivered it safely to Ethiopia. The Ethiopian church says they still have it and look after it to this day.

The music and dancing of Ethiopia are unique and differ from those of the West. The museums of our kings and queens are still preserved, and there is a statue of Emperor Hail Selassie, a revered figure among Rastafarians. The Ethiopian people are beautiful, kind, and caring towards each other. I was deeply moved by the culture that has existed for thousands of years, which is evident in the human bones of "Lucy."

Africa – The Horn of Africa

On my first trip to Africa, I visited Morocco. For my second and third trips, I went to Egypt, where I lived for a year. My fourth trip was to South Africa, where I was curious to learn about Mandela and see how the country had changed after he was released from prison. I wanted to explore the similarities between South African apartheid and the American Jim Crow system.

I landed in Cape Town and soon realized why whites didn't want to give up South Africa - it had the majestic Table Mountain. It was reminiscent of San Francisco, and I was amazed by it. During my stay, I saw traditional dancing in the plaza outside a mall. However, as New Year's approached, I decided to tour the city to understand the people and how they would treat me. Fortunately, I never had any issues.

However, one incident stands out. I went to a shop owned by a white person, and some local black people entered. I noticed that the owner was curt and generally not as nice with them as she was with me. She knew I was a foreigner, and it wasn't my imagination - she was very short with them. It was as if they didn't belong in such a nice shop. I decided to leave when she told them that there was nothing for them there. It was too much for me, and I left as well.

In general, I had a great time in South Africa. They have outdoor markets where vendors from different African countries come to sell their goods, including from neighboring Mozambique. I became familiar with Mozambicans and even traveled there. I arrived in Cape Town just before New Year's and found the city more beautiful than I expected, with a lot of Dutch influences in the buildings of the old sector.

Many of the buildings were not even 100 years old, and it was integrated. I didn't feel uncomfortable being black and didn't feel that my rights were being violated. However, there was one instance when I went into a bar and realized I was the only black person there. I didn't know whether to turn around and leave or stay. Despite this, I found the people generally very nice.

Despite feeling a bit uncomfortable at first, I went into the bar anyway and noticed another black guy there with a white guy. Although I initially felt uneasy, I soon made myself feel comfortable and had a drink. Since I wasn't there to meet anyone, I hung out and stayed for a while. Eventually, I felt more at ease and noticed the people around me seemed more relaxed as well. I suppose they weren't used to seeing a black person alone in their bar. Once they realized I wasn't a threat, they warmed up to me. I even had a pleasant conversation with a guy who came up to me while I was smoking outside.

Although I didn't have the same connections in Southern Africa as I did in other African countries, I still enjoyed exploring the downtown areas and the waterfront. While I didn't have the opportunity to visit people's homes in the countryside, I did get to experience the local life. Additionally, South Africa has become known for its wine, and many tourists now visit the vineyards for wine tours.

They have a cable car that takes you from The Cape Town Planes up to the mountains, which was quite interesting. I also wanted to visit Johannesburg and continue north to Victoria Falls, but I didn't get the chance. So, I decided to go to Mozambique instead.

When I got to the capital city of Maputo in Mozambique, I found that it was well-planned and I enjoyed my time there, especially during their street festival. I didn't do much, but I did try to explore the landscape, including visiting a jungle area. To get there, we took a small eight-seater plane to a resort area, where we were picked up in a station wagon with a compartment for passengers and our luggage on the back. We rode through the bushes and arrived at a village where I saw something new to me. The ladies in the market were selling their goods while sitting on the ground and chatting with each other.

I also met some guys there who lived in a hut while I lived in a resort area. We became friendly. I had my own bungalow. I had three meals a day. Breakfast was outside by the water. Lunch was also by the water. One night, they had the candles, the tiki lights, and all of that by the water. It was nice and touristy. I wanted it to feel a little more local. I took a bottle of Jack Daniels out the gate and met up with these guys I knew. We set up in a hut and ate whatever canned food that was there. We were doing Jack Daniels shots, eating, and talking. We were speaking in English, Portuguese, with a great deal of translating mixed in. They were young and it was a fun time. After maybe a couple of hours, I crawled back through the gated security to the private resort where I was staying. I felt very good going back, it was not that far, and I felt safe. I slept it off.

During the day, I explored the local village outside the resort where people went about their daily lives, selling their wares in huts and under trees. It was a colorful and vibrant environment, and I spent more time outside the resort than inside where the activities mainly consisted of sunbathing, swimming, and eating.

However, my first jungle experience in Africa was not what I expected as I didn't see the animals I had hoped for.

Hawaii - Pictures of Paradise

I was living comfortably in San Francisco until the building owner caught wind of me smoking weed during a low-key party with friends. She called the police and asked me to move out, which was quite unsettling. Thankfully, my friend came to the rescue. He invited me to stay with him and help with the event in Hawaii, which was a win-win situation for both of us.

Calvin Campbell

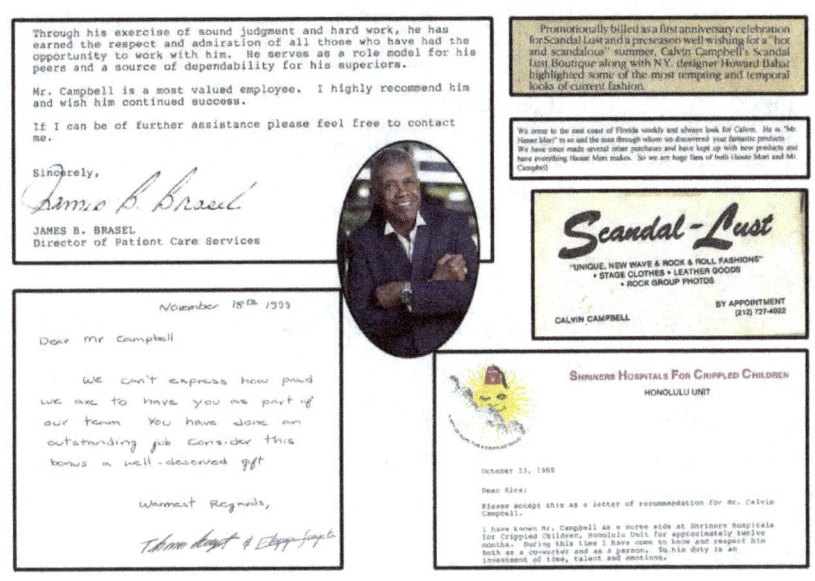

When I visited Hawaii, my main goal was to be a tourist and see Diamond Head in Waikiki. However, prior to opening Pictures of Paradise with Perry, I volunteered at the Shriners Children's Orthopedic Hospital in Waikiki. Children came from other Polynesian islands; Tonga, Western Samoa, even as far away as Korea to be helped. Some of the children spoke no English, but all needed someone to care for them while they were away from their parents. My experience was so effective that the hospital offered me a full-time job. Although I stayed only a year with the Shriners, I wanted to highlight this experience.

During my five year long stay in Hawaii, I also went windsurfing in Maui. It was my first time seeing it done up close, and I was amazed by the impressive tricks performed by skilled surfers. Although I wanted to visit Hawaii and the Big Island, my visit this time was brief as I had to return to New York to continue my freelance work.

During my time with Perry, I was impressed by his diligent work ethic and how he organized the event. As I observed him making early morning phone calls and following up on leads, I began thinking of ways to make more money from the event. Although Perry was paying me, I wanted to capitalize on the 12,000 people attending the event and increase my earnings.

People flocked to the Exotic Erotic Ball to let loose and enjoy the festivities. Attendees dressed in everything from skimpy outfits to elaborate fairytale costumes. The event boasted three live bands, Mr. Exotic Erotic, and various exotic edibles. I'll leave it at that.

With Perry's approval, I decided to sell disposable cameras at the event. Knowing that many people wouldn't bring their best cameras but would still want a souvenir, I sold exposed Kodak double cameras. It turned out to be a lucrative venture. Even if only 1,000 out of the 12,000 attendees purchased my cameras, it was still a success.

It took three months to plan the Exotic Erotic Ball, but Perry made a year's worth of income in just one month. Following the event, Perry's friend asked him to come to Hawaii to discuss a business idea to which Perry agreed. He returned with news that his friend managed an art gallery that spanned almost the entire second floor of the Hilton Hotel. His friend also proposed the idea for Perry to open a kiosk on the main street, where he could rent wall space to hang matted and framed pictures. Tourists passing by could view the well-lit artwork on display, including limited edition canvases and transferred canvases. Perry asked me privately if I could come and help him, as he couldn't do it alone.

179

I was living with Perry, who suggested that starting a business in Hawaii could be a profitable venture. Since he was footing the bill, I found the idea intriguing and was already prepared to leave. Perry specified that we would be heading to Waikiki, a prime tourist destination, rather than the capital, Honolulu. As Waikiki is home to the famous Waikiki Beach and attracts many influential people, I agreed and eagerly packed my bags.

Together, we planned and coordinated with Perry's friend to set up an outdoor art gallery in Waikiki. His friend found a suitable wall on the main street, adjacent to shops that sold various beach accessories, where many people walked by and liked what they saw and bought it. Perry rented the wall kiosk, which was visible from both directions, and made sure it was clean and painted. He sourced artwork from local Hawaiian artists, framed and duplicated them, and sold prints and limited editions at the outdoor gallery.

Japanese tourists often visit Hawaii for their honeymoon, anniversary, or vacation due to its proximity. The other significant group of tourists is from California, particularly from LA or San Diego, as it is not too far away. We also had visitors from all over the world, and there was always a lot of foot traffic, especially in the evening after the beach and before and after dinner. Our outdoor art gallery on the rented wall attracted people's attention, and we were able to replicate the concept of selling artwork and crafts seen in Paris on the Champs Elysees during their chandelier days. Our venture was very successful.

We were very successful because customers would visit during the day, before going to the beach, and inquire about the artwork. At night, the pieces were displayed in high-quality wooden frames under bright lights, allowing customers to envision them in their own homes. We set a minimum price of $35, and if customers wanted a canvas transfer, we could have it done within a day. For those leaving Hawaii, we took orders and shipped the artwork either "next day" or "two-day" delivery. Our business was so lucrative that we lived a lavish lifestyle, with a luxurious apartment boasting one of the only heated swimming pools, and we frequently hosted parties with plenty of women and fun.

We had a team of guys who took down the artwork at night and delivered it to our storage unit using our truck. The next morning, they returned with the artwork, and we set it up for another day of business. We operated seven days a week, but since we were located on the beach, I could take a break and enjoy the beach whenever I wanted, especially in the afternoons. I preferred working late evenings as we closed around 9:10 p.m. when the tourists were finished for the day and getting ready for dinner.

In some locations, there are small shops selling handmade crafts. The items sold are often very stylish and fashionable. If you're willing to spend a bit more, you can find more high-end items with brand labels.

Figure 44 The national parade honoring Queen Lili Uokalani, the first and last queen of Hawaii

Calvin Campbell

Canada

I have had the opportunity to visit two Canadian cities, Toronto, and Montreal They both left a lasting impression.

Toronto has a more laid-back atmosphere compared to bustling cities like New York or Boston, with a charm reminiscent of Philadelphia. I only stayed for a few days during a business trip, but the city's cleanliness and simplicity were appealing. Toronto's architecture is steeped in history, and although not extravagant, it has its own unique character.

Montreal, on the other hand, boasts a rich history and a strong French influence. The Old City area with its horse-drawn carriages and cobblestone streets, combined with the abundance of French restaurants, creates a distinct and charming ambiance. Despite my limited French vocabulary, I enjoyed the city's welcoming attitude towards people of color, Arabs, and Blacks. It's commendable that the Canadian government is working towards rectifying the situation of the indigenous people. Overall, Canada is a friendly neighbor, and both Toronto and Montreal are unique and worthwhile destinations to visit.

Exploring Asia

Following my success, I was able to take a trip to Thailand. Perry accompanied me and we spent some time together before heading to Bangkok, where we stayed for about a week. Bangkok was a bustling city, but I didn't find it very enjoyable as I didn't speak Thai and navigating around was challenging. Eventually, I decided to return to Thailand on my own, but avoided staying in Bangkok. Instead, I explored places like Chiang Mai, Kohsamu, Phuket, and other areas with beautiful beaches, a larger number of international tourists, and more entertaining activities.

If you're from Hawaii, you probably don't want to be stuck in a city. You'd prefer a similar environment. While living in Hawaii wasn't always fun and involved a lot of work, I had my days and nights free after working in the evenings. Although my job wasn't particularly difficult, it was essential to be present to avoid missing out on any customers. Fortunately, there was also a slow season in Hawaii, mostly towards the end of August, September, and October. During this time, I took the opportunity to travel, while Perry returned to San Francisco for the Exotic Erotic Ball.

Although I resided in Hawaii, I frequently embarked on small excursions. On separate occasions, I visited Thailand, went on to Indonesia, staying in Bali and Hubd for roughly two weeks and returning twice. I liked it so much I also traveled to Malaysia and

Seoul, South Korea. In Seoul there is an area called Etwan where the presence of American military personnel made it an enjoyable destination. I especially enjoyed the black clubs, where most black people went for the music and Korean girls who were interested in Americans and black music. I stayed and partied there because they played all the music from back home, and I felt a strong connection. Moreover, it was always a pleasure to see other Americans, especially black Americans.

To me, it doesn't matter whether someone is a member of the military or not. I'm always grateful to see black people traveling and experiencing different cultures. We shouldn't limit ourselves to our own little worlds, and I'm glad that we are generally welcomed wherever we go, as long as we behave respectfully. Of the 60 countries I've visited and the 10 countries I've lived in, I can't recall a time when I felt uncomfortable, or had a bad experience.

People are usually kind and treat you based on how you present yourself. If you come across as aggressive or superior, they may be distant. However, in general, I had a fantastic experience during my travels.

Indonesia was amazing. I stayed in Hbud, another location in Indonesia where various artists displayed their art, including many types of paintings. In northern Indonesia, there is a unique art culture, and I witnessed a special dance that involved clicking.

In Bali where I stayed, Hbud has been home to many royal families. Bali has wonderful landscapes, beaches, mountains, and flourishing of street, and craft centers all over the city. Many of the shops have great displays. They have a vibrant spiritual culture. Bali is enjoyable and caters to people who are welcoming.

The locals in Indonesia are deeply immersed in their culture, evident in their many outdoor theaters and cultural events. When attending these events, I truly appreciated their grace and togetherness. While Malaysia was a bit too religious for my liking, I am always open to experiencing different religions. However, if I cannot be myself, it is time to move on. Thailand, on the other hand, is always a good time.

After my Asian trip to South Korea, Thailand, Indonesia, and Malaysia, I returned to Hawaii to focus on work. As Halloween came to an end, we began preparing for the fall season and introducing our work. However, there was always time for a good party. Clubs in Waikiki and restaurants hosted many famous people, including Dolly Parton. Independence Day in Hawaii was a sight to behold, with Waikiki and Honolulu illuminated with festivities and celebration. The history of Hawaii is one that should be explored, as it is a story of American colonialism and the unjust treatment of the Hawaiian queen. Despite this, my time in Hawaii was filled with some of the best experiences in America. I always say aloha, and mahala.

I experienced a difficult situation when my father called to tell me about my stepmother's passing. I headed back home for the funeral. However, my parents no longer resided in the Bronx nor Harlem where I grew up; instead, they had moved to Queens. Just like other families, they desired a place with a backyard, picket fence, and peaceful neighborhood, which led them to buy a house in Cambria Heights, Long Island. Although I would visit them, it was not a place for me to stay for an extended period.

I returned to New York to support my father in arranging the funeral. It was a time when my big Southern family came together to sing and pray. There were mixed feelings on both sides about my stepmother, and some people embraced her while others embraced my father. After the funeral, I left my father with my relatives there since he could handle his own stuff. However, I was concerned about him because he had a reputation being a player and attracting women. Even though he didn't drink. He smoked cigarettes and slept a lot, and being alone after his wife's death, it was important to be cautious about people who might take advantage of him.

To make a long story short, I went back to Hawaii. I was thinking of my father because I left home at 18 years old. my father and I never really had the man to man. When my stepmother died, I kept calling him to make sure he was okay. He said, "Yeah," he was okay. He was doing his thing.

My father was very heavy, and he had poor circulation in his legs. I was worried about him, because my father was on his own in a house with a basement and lots of stairs. I was concerned about his ability to manage himself and his affairs. I decided to move back to New York. Because I found in life that all you have are your parents when it comes down to who loves you unconditionally. My father was a good guy, a hard worker, and I just didn't want to miss the opportunity of spending quality time with him. Now that the wicked witch was dead, I was very emotional about it.

Now that the Wicked Witch was died, and he was alone I was very emotional about it. My stepmom had always made me look bad in front of him. There was no love between her and me.

I had never forgiven her for her spiteful actions and control over me. At thirteen I had made friends with a family that lived up on the fourth floor, I used to take back their bottles for cash and help carry their groceries upstairs. The mother and two daughters would talk to me and sometimes give me a soda, they liked my help. Sometimes when I was there a man would visit with them in the kitchen, it didn't take me long to realize he was the famous guitar player Bo Diddly. I was such a fan of his, I was always thrilled when he was visiting them and spoke to me. One day he said he had an old guitar, and would I like it, I was so excited I could hardly speak to answer. The next time he visited his kinfolk he brought me the guitar; I flew home so happy. Guitar in hand I burst in on my stepmother talking away telling her the story. My stepmom demanded I return it at once. With a devastated heavy heart, I took it back up to the fourth floor. The most exciting and incredible thing that had happened to me in my short life the wicked witch tore apart for no reason. This experience taught me two things: one I lost all respect I had for her. Secondly: I realized that she was purposely cruel.

My father was a hardworking man who never let us go without. He worked on the waterfront as a longshoreman, and it was because of him we had a comfortable life. So, I made a deal with Perry to sell out, and I decided to return to New York with the money I earned.

New York

Coming back to New York was a major decision for me, but it turned out to be one of the best decisions I've ever made. It wasn't motivated by money, but rather by my love for my father. To me, nothing was more important than spending time with him, especially as he was getting older. I didn't have a clear plan when I made the decision to return, but I knew it was the right thing to do.

In Queens, where I lived with my dad, I was still able to connect with many friends from my earlier years. Although it took me nearly an hour to get to work in Manhattan by bus and subway, I still made the daily journey to Lord and Taylor on 5th Avenue. I didn't have a car and didn't want to take my father's car since parking in New York can be a hassle, and I didn't want to risk getting parking tickets.

Because I was going through a tough time, I reached out to some of my educated friends for advice. Although most of them didn't have the same lifestyle as me, one of my military friends who traveled frequently offered some useful insight. They suggested that I find a career that would allow me to support my love for travel and could be done anywhere in the world. The surprising suggestion was to become a hairdresser. Initially, I didn't think it was a good fit for me since I disliked taking care of my own hair. However, my friends clarified that I didn't have to become a hairdresser, but getting a license would enable me to open a salon and manage other hairdressers who had their own customers.

My friends also suggested that I consider becoming an esthetician, a skincare specialist, by going back to school. They pointed out that most black people do hair, but few specialize in skincare. Many black people don't feel that white establishments understand their skin type and, therefore, prefer to go to black-owned establishments for skincare. Additionally, there's a lack of males specializing in skincare. This presented a unique opportunity for me to have my own product and tap into an underserved market. Although it was a surprising suggestion, I realized that it was a practical way to support my love for travel and maintain my lifestyle.

My friends suggested that learning American skincare techniques would be beneficial as it's considered more technically advanced than French skincare education. Moreover, since Americans are good at copying, I would have various options to learn and gain a competitive advantage, especially in New York, where there's ample opportunity to observe the competition and understand the industry. Initially, I was skeptical, but the more I considered it, the more appealing it became.

I discussed this idea with my father, who didn't fully comprehend it at first. Nevertheless, he has always been supportive and encouraged me to pursue it if I thought I could make a living out of it. He even offered to cover my expenses for the time being. My father has always taken care of me, and I'm grateful for his unwavering support.

However, some people in the neighborhood gossiped about my lifestyle, including my frequent travels and being unmarried. My father promptly put them in their place and defended me. I heard about this from my relatives, my father's friends, and even his neighbors. I'm blessed to have such a supportive and protective father. He defended me with, "He has traveled the world, never caused me any problems, never been in jail, and I love my son. I wish I could have done what he did when I was his age."

During dinner, my father and I talked about my life and my plans. It was the first time he ever told me that he loved me and accepted me for who I am. Hearing those words from him made me feel liberated and empowered. I didn't care what anyone else thought because my father's approval was all I needed. He understood my lifestyle, my love for travel, and my artistic pursuits. He never judged me for my clothes or hairstyles and allowed me to be myself. I am grateful for him and feel blessed to have him as my father. It's a reminder that God always gives us what we need in life.

Figure 45 Calvin Campbell, Sr (Dad) & Calvin Campbell, Jr (me), visiting family

Figure 46 Thomas Campbell, my grandfather born January 3, 1897, died May 16, 1978

Cosmetology School & Esthetics

I am grateful for the girls in my class who helped me with roller sets, color, and pin curls because it wasn't my forte. As one of the only three guys in a class of around 30 girls, I felt appreciated and celebrated. They helped us because they enjoyed it, and even though I was just there to get my degree, it was a pleasant experience. After finishing school, I took a break and went back to Hawaii to check on my friend Perry and our art gallery, Pictures of Paradise.

I went back to see Perry because I realized he couldn't manage the gallery alone, even with employees. There were many things to keep track of, including inventory. He told me he was considering closing the gallery since it wasn't his original idea and therefore not his top priority. The gallery wasn't open as much as it would have been if I were there. Unfortunately, while we were struggling, another group opened a similar concept in the mall and people took advantage of our shortcomings. Another group opened a similar shop downtown, selling prints, transfers, and reproductions, and it became popular.

Calvin Campbell

Living in St Petersburg Florida

I relocated to St. Petersburg, Florida because I had previously spent two months living in St. Petersburg, Russia one summer. I've been living in Florida for three years now and it has been a wonderful place to live. I feel blessed to have found such a beautiful home with a stunning view from my balcony where I can watch manatees, baby sharks, dolphins, and other types of wild fish. When I decided to move here, three dolphins appeared, two on one side and one on the other side of the harbor, which was a sign to me that I am still favored.

Although I had heard about hurricane season, which typically lasts from July to November, I had never experienced one before. However, in October 2022, Hurricane Ian hit our area. Initially, Tampa Bay, including St. Petersburg, was preparing for a direct hit from the hurricane, but the storm changed course and devastated other nearby communities instead. I was worried about the possibility of water entering my living space through the all-glass windows, but thankfully, my home was unscathed.

My thoughts were that birds can tell when a hurricane is coming, because all the birds were leaving as the weather was changing. I saw the clouds approaching, but I wasn't sure what signal the birds were giving. I certainly did not understand they were signaling that something of that magnitude was about to happen.

I was told that night, that not since a hurricane hit Tarpon Springs in 1921 has Tampa Bay has a direct hit by any major storm.

I was also told by locals that no other hurricane is known to have made a direct hit on Tampa Bay after the *cyclone* of 1863 which made landfall in Clearwater, Florida in late September over 150 years ago. There's a local legend that mounds-built years ago by a certain Native American tribe protects the area from major storms.

Figure 47 Standing on the beach at The Don Cesar

Living in St. Petersburg, Florida has been great for me, and it's no coincidence that I chose to move here since I had previously lived in St. Petersburg, Russia for a couple of months during the summer. I feel so blessed to have found such a beautiful place to call home. When I was considering moving here, three dolphins showed up in the harbor, which I took as a sign of good luck.

With my blessings, I look forward to my next adventure, which happens to be an invitation from one of my best friends to celebrate his 50th birthday in Kenya in April. I'm excited to explore Nairobi, Mombasa, and other parts of the country with its rich East African history. It's not for a wedding or funeral, but just a celebration, which makes it more special. Anyone interested in joining me is welcome.

Figure 48 Freelance work in Tampa, in International Mall

Figure 49 Standing in front one of my favorite restaurants.

Figure 50 Standing among trees in St. Petersburg

Calvin Campbell

Humanity Love and Compassion

As someone who has traveled extensively, I have many stories to share about humanity, love, and compassion. I believe it's important to give back and express my gratitude for all the kindness and respect that people of different colors, nationalities, and religions have shown me throughout my travels. I feel incredibly fortunate to now be living in Florida, where I can show my appreciation for the blessings in my life and the supportive community around me. Growing up in Manhattan, New York, specifically South Bronx, has also influenced my perspective and appreciation for diversity.

In New York City, you have the opportunity to connect and interact with people from all over the world who come from different backgrounds. It makes you curious about their origins and how they bring their unique cultures and interests with them. As you learn about their experiences, you start to realize that you share common joys and struggles.

My own interest in global influences was sparked when I was a kid growing up in New York City. I remember watching television and being captivated by Emperor Haile Selassie, who was speaking at the United Nations. His presence was awe-inspiring, not just for my family and community, but for the entire city. What really amazed me was when he moved his entire entourage from downtown to Harlem. It was the first time I had seen a black king or prince from Africa, and it left a lasting impression on me.

Calvin Campbell

Live a Dream You Never Knew Existed

We've all heard it, travel when you're older and you've saved for retirement:

But travel often require good health, which you likely have right now.

If you have dreams to see the world, don't you owe it to yourself to realize them?

We understand that life interjects, and bills pile up, but, when you look back at your life in five years, what do you want to see?

Figure 51 Calvin and Grandma Laura Peake Campbell

I came from a good southern family and Grandmother Laura was my rock. You had to show respect; "Yes sir." "No ma'am." After my mother died, I stayed with my grandparents for several years in Virginia until my father remarried. I had other cousins living there too. We were a big family in a big house. Somehow, we all fit. At Grandmas, a woman couldn't swear, drink, smoke, or dress in a provocative manner. Miss Laura Campbell didn't play. She was the backbone of the entire family. She had twelve children, two died at birth but she was always there for us. God bless my loving grandma.

What's Next? Panama Again? Why?

As a senior citizen, I have found Panama to be a good option for my next destination. However, it's important to remember that every place has its own time and season in life's journey, and there are many other places to enjoy besides Panama. After living and working there for seven years, I am now returning to the United States.

When it comes to retirement, selecting the perfect destination requires thoughtful consideration of various factors. Luckily, Panama provides all the benefits of retiring abroad without the high costs. To get a feel for the location, it's important to explore popular retirement tour services and even plan a short holiday. Ultimately, the ideal retirement spot should feel like the ultimate vacation, which is precisely what Panama offers.

P.S. I also dream of my time in Ethiopia with inspiration, admiration and hope for our people.

Figure 52 Iguana looking for food near my home in Panama.

I Am Blessed

I've been blessed and highly favored living my passion, my life journey, and sharing it with others. I am still living my blessed life and I'm truly thankful! The power of following your passion of UBU ME B ME and staying close to God and his power of showing so much beauty around the world.

I've been blessed with a great friend. I would like to thank Marion Runacre for her friendship, support, and help with proofreading.

You must depend on God's hand and watch God change things in your mind and surroundings such that you can move forward.

Over the years, music has been my inspiration and in some cases, my support. It kept me going as a global nomadic traveler. Here are some of my favorites:

Can't Give Up Now	Mary Mary
You Know Me	George Huff
Alone But Not Alone	Marvin Winans
Here I Am To Worship	William Mc Dowell
I Want To Say Thank you	Lisa Page Brooks
Thank you For it all	Marvin Sapp
A Brighter Day	George Huff
Just Don't Wanna Know	Marvin Winans
I Wonder What It's Like to Be Free	Nina Simone
Jerusalema	Master KG NomceboZika
One Day	Matisyahu

BE BLESSED

Calvin Campbell, The Global Nomad

Ambition reached or dreams put out to dry.

INSHALLAH
If God Willing

GYE NYAME
(JEH-N-YAH-MEE)
The Supremacy of God

Shalom (Peace)

There But For
The Grace of God, Go I